THE JOY OF GOD

THE JOY
OF GOD

H. A. Williams, C.R.

Templegate Publishers / Springfield, Illinois

First published in Great Britain by
Mitchell Beazley Publishers Ltd., London

U.S. edition published 1979 by
Templegate Publishers
302 East Adams Street
Springfield, Illinois 62701

ISBN 0-87243-092-8

CONTENTS

PREFACE

I have sub-titled this book "Variations on a Theme" because it repeats itself. Such repetition is, I believe, inevitable. You would have to be a saint to know the Joy of God in anything approaching human adequacy. To the ordinary person God's Joy is known only in shreds and patches; and therefore it will inevitably be the same shreds and patches that will be assembled in different patterns and linked up with various areas of association. The worlds of selfhood, of other people, of nature, and of the arts recur frequently, though each time (such at least has been my intention) in a slightly different context. Another recurring theme is that the experience of God's Joy is not confined to people belonging to the closed shop of any ecclesiastical trade union. For it seems to me that what many Christians find hardest of all to believe is that the wind bloweth where it listeth.

I am profoundly grateful to James Mitchell for suggesting that I should write about the Joy of God. If little may be discovered from reading this book, a great deal has been discovered from writing it.

H. A. W.

"Ah yes, I was missing that, and I don't want to miss it. I love that passage: it's Cana of Galilee, the first miracle. Ah, that miracle! Ah, that sweet miracle! It was not men's grief but their joy Christ visited. He worked His first miracle to help men's gladness."

Fyodor Dostoevsky, *The Brothers Karamazov*

THE TRICKY CUSTOMER

Joy is a tricky customer. It seldom allows you to know where you are.

It can, for instance, gate-crash into your life like an overpowering guest who dominates everything and begins to make you feel displaced. Indeed it can so threaten to eat you up that your instincts of self-preservation are aroused and you begin to resist it on the plea of being overwrought. Is it pleasure or pain? You hardly know. Certainly it isn't comfort. Comfort spells security, and joy can take you out of yourself to a degree where all security is left far behind. You are no longer in control. Joy has invaded and conquered you; will it end by destroying you? Behind the initial feeling of exultation you sense the flame of incandescent terror. You seek to protect yourself with the nearest cliché at hand: "Enough", you say, "is enough"—even when your visitor is exceeding gladness and delight.

It is the kind of experience usually associated with the sudden impinging upon us of some aspect of transcendent reality. It is as though we were caught up in the blaze of eternity. But the experience can also on occasion spring from very much more homely and mundane roots:

"Will it ever cloy?
This odd diversity of misery and joy,
I'm feeling quite insane
And young again
And all because I'm mad about the boy."

(Noel Coward)

It is the experience Ibsen unfolded in *The Master Builder*.

On the other hand, joy can be an unseen guest, its presence unrecognized until it has left or threatened to leave. Perhaps joy is most profoundly ours when it is thus with us unawares. For then we receive it without knowing what we're doing and hence without resistance. At the time when joy was ours all we were aware of was not itself but what brought it: somebody with us we loved; the view or music which entranced us; the deeper understanding which came to us as we read or studied; the growing mastery of some practical art like cooking or accountancy; or the relaxation of being among friends we knew well and could trust. It is when these occasions of joy have passed and we compare them with our present circumstances that we are aware of our former joy. The classic instance of this is the widowed spouse, but it can take all sorts of forms: "I didn't know how lucky I was."

Joy can also make us aware of its presence by threatening to leave: Does she still love me? Am I growing insensitive to music? What shall I feel like when I've been in this job for ten years? This heavenly holiday—we've got less than a week more of it. Joy makes itself felt by the discovery of anxiety as its bed-fellow. And the anxiety that identifies the joy begins to spoil it.

This can happen with regard to the future no less than the present. We can look forward to joy: somebody's arrival, an inviting task, a treat of some kind or other. But the more industriously we make arrangements for joy, the more carefully we set the stage for its entrance, the more is our anticipation of it mixed with foreboding. Perhaps joy will ignore our invitation altogether or arrive in some mutilated form, which will disappoint more than it pleases. And since we tend to be intolerant of suspense, often something within us almost forces us to spoil the occasion outright and have done with it, throwing all our careful preparations down the drain, as we persuade ourselves and try to persuade others that what we said or did wasn't meant to be aggressive in the slightest. Thus are we aware of future joy by the possibility of its absence or of its being far from unmixed and total.

Sometimes joy teases us by playing with us a game of "If only": if only Smith weren't one of my colleagues; if only the mortgage rate would go down; if only Betty would be more considerate when I got home; if only John would sometimes think of me instead of himself; if only the children occasionally did well at school; if only I didn't get touches of backache. If only this or that condition were fulfilled, my joy would be complete. In varying degrees we allow ourselves to be subjected to the tortures of Tantalus, making joy into a near relative of the Father of Lies. And in this role joy has yet another trick up its sleeve: it can persuade us that it lives happily with almost everybody except ourselves. Look at the others joining exhilaratingly in the dance of life while I am in a cramp. Poor me! There is nothing like the fantasied joys of others to induce self-pity.

It was no exaggeration, then, to describe joy as a tricky customer. It can threaten to overpower or even destroy us. It is unseen when most fully possessed. It is most often recognized when it has gone or when mixed with anxiety about its departure. It can poison the future with suspense. It can tease us with deceptions about ourselves and others. And withal it is a will-o'-the-wisp, incalculable in its behaviour, one of life's great uncertainties, except that it can always be relied on to leave, its hand ever at its lips bidding adieu.

POWDERED JOY

The use made of words reveals people's attitude to what the words indicate. In English (which includes American) usage there are growing signs that people have got fed up with reserving the word "joy" exclusively or even mainly for an emotion so incalculable, so out of control, as joy in its traditional sense. We want joy as something definite and concrete, which is at least possible for us to grasp at will and over which we can in principle exercise mastery. Hence we have expanded our use of the word "joy" to include precisely that.

In popular parlance it can refer to the achievement of a limited and particular result. You have been tinkering with the car all the afternoon trying to mend the clutch, and on coming in for tea your wife asks you: "Any joy?" meaning "Have you succeeded in mending it?"

Some sort of innate pessimism makes our use of "joy" in this sense chiefly negative. So, if we have tried to get the boss to agree to a proposal, it is unlikely that we shall describe our success as "joy", but we may well describe our failure by saying "No joy".

And in slang at least the word has been extended to mean a result which is certain, as when a taker of illegal drugs is described as a joy-popper and alcohol as joy-juice.

Such contemporary usages may seem insignificant, but then a man can be convicted of murder by a finger-print. People want to think and speak of joy as something they can manage, to rob it of its elusive quality and thus become its master.

FISH OUT OF WATER

In playing with words people reveal what they want, but no word-game can change what is in fact the case. Joy as gladness and delight remains the tricky customer it always was, at best no better than an erratic and inconstant lover, seldom behaving as it should.

Of course we can try to protect ourselves against its vagaries by, as we say, getting down to work and thinking of other things, joining the ranks of those

"... strained time-ridden faces
Distracted from distraction by distraction
Filled with fancies and empty of meaning."*

But it is hard to keep that up all the time. Truth, we may reluctantly have to admit, is mighty and will prevail. And one of the central truths about ourselves is that while somewhere within us we know that we were made for joy, at the same time we also know that our purchase upon it is, to say the least, tenuous. And so we feel the deadening bitterness of that "division between the mind that desires and the world which disappoints". Camus could not have stated more succinctly the grief of joy and the grievance it occasions. The grief and grievance of joy equates life with endless dissatisfaction, making

*Notes and references are gathered at the back of the book on pp. 129–35.

us feel like a Cinderella whose fairy-godmother seldom appears, and when she does is the very reverse of reliable. Too much too soon, too little too late, bankruptcy, a total lack of consistency, jam yesterday and jam tomorrow but never jam today—we can hurl the whole stale vocabulary of political vituperation against the grief and grievance of joy.

There is, of course, nothing new in this dismal diagnosis. It has always been apparent to people who had the courage to think. Plato described it (to use the roughest outline) as our being caught in the limitation between un-being and being; half-illusory and half-real; if you like, half-dead and half-alive. St Augustine, the greatest of Plato's legatees, at the very beginning of the first autobiography ever written, summed up the situation in words which became famous: "Thou hast made us for Thyself and our hearts are restless until they find rest in Thee."

THE HOLE IN THE HEART

There is nothing morbid or sick in a person's experience of the grief of joy any more than in a person's experience of toothache. It is the tooth which is sick, not the ache. The ache, by showing painfully the true condition of the tooth, is a protest against it and thus a drive towards health. Similarly the pressures within us which force us to recognize joy as a cruelly tricky customer are healthy indicators that things with us are not as they should be, that our own true identity is somehow eluding us, that we have only by fits and starts (if even that) what, we intuitively recognize, should really belong to us fully as a permanent possession. Because our joy is so uncertain and spasmodic we realize that we live a half-in-half existence, partly within our element and partly out of it.

The diagnosis could be enlarged thus: it is natural for us always to want more—more love, more prestige, more money, more everything. But it is easy for us to miss the inner thrust of this desire for more and imagine that it could in the end be satisfied by the accumulation of riches of every kind and variety; not just possessions in the ordinary sense (few of us are silly enough for that) but rewards such as consideration, recognition, gratitude, affection and respect. We think that if others gave us enough of these we should be satisfied. But our wanting more in fact goes deeper than anything that our earthly environment can supply, and we misunderstand it if we imagine it can finally be appeased by what this limited world can give us. For our desire is literally insatiable, which means that it belongs to the order of infinity. Our always wanting more is the way in which we clumsily express our intuition that we were made for what is endless and without bounds, that is, for God.

When our pursuit of satisfaction becomes hectic, a restless search for, say, power or sex or pleasure or work and more work, then **we** may be sure that we are blindly attempting the impossible, failing to recognize that the human heart is greater than all that is not God.

> "No single station of the globe
> Can rest the urgency of love,
> Whose true vocation must exceed
> All pastures where its children feed,
> Transcending in one breathless act
> The possibilities of fact,
> We learn no mortal creature is
> The end of love's immensities."

THE FREE MARKET

Once we have recognized that our desire exceeds everything in this earthly historical order and that in our hearts we pass beyond the limits of our given world, once, in short, we become aware that we were made for God and that nothing less than God can satisfy us, then what more obvious course for us than to go out and get Him?

He is, after all, widely advertised and offered for

sale by a variety of firms, most of which call themselves churches, though some call themselves
movements and campaigns. Indeed once we go out
to shop we find ourselves suffering from a daunting
embarras de richesse, and we may think it a pity that
consumer advice organizations don't examine the
various gods on the market and advise us about the
best buy.

It is true that brand loyalty has decreased considerably over the past two or three decades. But it
can still be found, though by now it is generally of
the silent and implicit kind rather than the crudely
vocal. That the Catholic or Protestant God is the
best is tacitly assumed rather than openly stated,
while the Anglican finds ways of implying that his
God combines the advantages of both, thus giving
what the advertisers call double value. Within the
last ten or fifteen years Dionysus also has re-
appeared in the markets of Christendom, baptized
with a Christian name, while the revivalist God—
half-bully, half-sugar-daddy—seems to appear
regularly on the scene brandishing his cane and his
candy. Meanwhile foreign competition has grown
considerably, with Eastern religions flooding the
market like Japanese cars.

The trouble with gods when they are thus ex-
hibited for sale is that they become no more than a
line of consumer goods and are as limited and earth-
bound as any of the other things of this world.
What, of course, is limited is not necessarily their
essential character—what in deepest truth they

are—but the attitude and approach we are encouraged to make to them. We are invited to treat them as entities we can acquire like gramophone records. And of a god so acquired perhaps the most realistic if brutal estimate is that of Stendhal's young hero Julien Sorel, who, in the face of the inconstancy of his mistress, mutters to himself: "What's the use of a love like this? One might as well take to religion."

For it belongs to the gods that are for sale to offer instant and more or less continuous pleasure, whether it be the pleasure of excitement or of tranquillization. And not only those pleasures either, but goodies like success, happiness, freedom from distress, and in general health and wealth. We are reminded of Mrs Whittaker (who, unlike her sister, married well) in Dorothy Parker's short story:

> "Mrs Whittaker's attitude of kindly tolerance was not confined to her less fortunate relatives. It extended to friends of her youth, working people, the arts, politics, the United States in general and God, who had always supplied her with the best of service. She could have given Him an excellent reference at any time."

But when the god fails to deliver the goods, be it excitement, tranquillization, well-being or whatever, he is dropped—thrown away like a broken gadget. And even when he does keep what is considered his side of the bargain, he leaves hunger in the heart (all the worse for being smothered) as all things of this earth alone are bound to do. Religion as a species of insurance, sedation or joy-popping cannot fail to betray its devotees.

It is bracing to turn from these gods for sale (which are no gods) to the testimony of a man of profound religious insight and devotion, a high authority on Christian mysticism, Friedrich von Hügel, who wrote towards the end of his long life:

> "Religion has never made me happy; it's no use shutting your eyes to the fact that the deeper you go, the more alone you will find yourself. . . . Religion has never made me comfy. I have been in the desert ten years. All deepened life is deepened suffering, deepened dreariness, deeper joy. Suffering and joy. The final note of religion is joy."

DISCOVERY

God is not for sale. He cannot be bought. In spite of appearances to the contrary, the churches, when true to themselves, know that they are not stalls at Vanity Fair and that all they can do is encourage people to discover the true God for themselves. People can do this because, as St Paul is reported to have said at Athens: "God is not far from each one of us, for in Him we live and move and have our being." If ultimately only God can satisfy our infinite longing, only He fill the hole in our heart, it might look as if we had to set out on a desperate search for Him. And because the words of earth can only most indirectly and obliquely indicate the realities of heaven, there is a sense in which we do indeed have to search for God, to seek if we are to find, to knock if it is to be opened to us. But it is an odd sort of searching, for it ends with the discovery that God is and has been with us all the time, that He is not far off, but nearer to us than the air we breathe, and that, like the air, His presence with us is not something we have earned, but is a free gift to all. Because we can speak of God only obliquely, in our talk about Him we shall get tied up in all sorts of inconsistent spatial metaphors. That doesn't matter. What godly men try to tell us makes sense in spite of the apparent contradictions.

We discover God as our environment. In the homely imagery of the psalmist, He is about our path and about our bed and familiar with all our ways. It is in Him, to quote St Paul again, that we live and move and have our being. But if God is around us He is also within us. And if He is within us it is not as an alien, not as Another, but as our truest selves. A human individual with a powerful personality may be said to invade us as an alien, destroying our autonomy and forcing us into his own mould so that we lose our own identity and become mere copies of his. The same thing happens on the rare occasions when sexual passion reaches a pitch of almost demonic proportions as when Catherine Earnshaw says to her old nurse: "Nellie, I *am* Heathcliff."

But unlike another human being, God is our creator, and by dwelling within us He makes us our own true selves and establishes our personal identity. He negates Himself in us in order to find Himself in us. That is to say, He limits Himself so that, instead of overwhelming us, He gradually and gently calls forth into being the tender, vulnerable fragility of our true selfhood, the fragility which when made perfect is also stronger than steel. And in this continuous creative work within us, which is His presence, it is Himself which He discovers in us. "God begins to live in me," says Thomas Merton, "not only as my creator but as my other and true self"—other and true because I spend much of my time fabricating a false self instead of allowing God to create me.

When we consider God's relationship to the self we are often misled by concentrating too exclusively on one particular spatial metaphor. God is above us, we say. Well, from one point of view, of course He is above us, infinitely so. He is our creator and there is an infinite difference between God and what He creates. But God's relationship to us is not an outside relationship in which He is in one place and we in another. As our creator God is the ground of our being, the fount from which we continually flow. The self I am is constituted by its relationship to God as its deepest centre. If God gives us the gift of infinite difference from Himself, He also gives us the gift of identity with Himself, a truth summarized by St Paul in his statement: "I live; yet not I, but Christ liveth in me." "God utters me like a word containing a partial thought of Himself. . . . If I am true to the concept God utters in me, if I am true to the thought of Him I was meant to embody, I shall be full of His actuality and find Him everywhere in myself." It is a truth which can bear emphasizing as it comes strangely to many Christians. Let us therefore listen to the seventeenth-century Catholic mystic—he was a Pole—Angelus Silesius:

> "Stop, where dost thou run?
> God's heaven is in thee.
> If thou seekest it elsewhere
> Never shalt thou see!

> "In good time we shall see
> God and His light you say!
> Fool, never shall you see
> What you don't see today."

Or we could listen to the down-to-earth eighteenth-century Jesuit Jean Pierre de Caussade, who wrote:

> "Truly, said Jacob, God is in this place and I knew it not. You seek God and He is everywhere; everything proclaims Him, everything gives Him to you. He walks by your side, is around you and within you: there He lives, and yet you seek Him.

You seek your own idea of God while all the time you possess Him substantially [i.e. in fullest possible reality]."

If God so made us that only He Himself can ultimately satisfy us, He does not withhold that gift of Himself. It is ours already, but, being too blind to recognize it, we have to discover it, not in religious theory, but in the warmth and sweetness and dryness and terror of actual living.

In our discovery of God's gift of Himself to us we discover a lot of less pleasant things as well. Hence von Hügel's talk of loneliness and deserts, deepened dreariness, and deepened joy; suffering and joy, with the final note of joy. But discussion of those crucial topics will be reserved for a special section later (page 94). We shall now consider God's relationship with the world as well as with ourselves. "The earth is the Lord's and the fullness thereof." How?

GOD ABOVE, AROUND AND WITHIN

Transcendence and Immanence

We have already noticed the trouble caused by the spatial metaphors we have to use when we talk of God. They have bedevilled our understanding of God's relationship with His world.

We have first of all to say that God is infinitely above the world He creates, that He is fully Himself without it; in other words that He is transcendent. As the creator we have to say that He is behind His creation holding it up, continuously keeping it in being. But we have also to say that He is within His creation, filling every part of it. It is the last statement which causes some Christians unnecessary anxiety. For they imagine that it implies that God is identical with the universe without remainder, coterminous with it, so that with Spinoza we can say God or Nature, it doesn't matter which. The implication is (as Coleridge pointed out) that when we say "It's cold" or "It's raining" we might as well say "God's cold" or "God's raining". We can, however, believe that God indwells His universe, filling every part of it, without pantheistic assumptions of that kind. God can still be above and behind for all His being within. As Christian orthodoxy has always asserted, if God is transcendent He is also immanent. In fact, when you look at it, you find that transcendence and immanence are one and the same thing. Professor Ninian Smart has summarized this very clearly:

> "If transcendence means that God is not spatial, and yet is distinct from the cosmos while sustaining it, so to say, from behind, then there is no strong reason to distinguish this account of transcendence from one main meaning of immanence. The belief that God works *within* all things merely uses a different spatial analogy from the belief that He is behind or beyond the cosmos."

Charles Davis has acutely observed that without the apprehension of God's immanence we can no longer recognize Him as transcendent. When God was no longer perceived as the ground and deepest centre of all things, when the experience of His immanence was thus lost, "God became only an object, over against the [perceiving] subject, an object among other objects. The loss of immanence destroyed true transcendence. Only its semblance remained in the placing of God as an object at an infinite distance [from His world]." In the event God as object disappeared beyond the horizon altogether and people ceased to believe in Him. For, as Dom Aelred Graham has said, people need "an explanation of human life less remote than that provided by a power outside the system, a God beyond the sky".

God is within the world, we can say, as its ultimate mystery. And to be aware of the mystery is to be aware of God. The discovery of God in ourselves and in all things does not mean the discovery of some definable entity (of which the old man in the sky is the *reductio ad absurdum*). A definable entity would not be God. Discovering God in ourselves and in all things means sensing the presence of mystery everywhere, mystery which evokes wonder, love, awe, tenderness, terror, interest, fascination —mystery.

> "Whose dwelling is the light of setting suns,
> And the round ocean and the living air,
> And the blue sky, and in the mind of man:
> A motion and a spirit that impels
> All thinking things, all objects of all thought
> And rolls through all things."

Russian Christianity was (and still is) deeply aware of God's presence in the world of nature and man. In *A Raw Youth* Dostoevsky has wonderfully expressed this awareness in the character of Makar Ivanovitch, a peasant who is an old man when the novel opens. Makar speaks of a person "filled full with days, yearning for his last hour, and rejoicing when he is gathered as an ear of wheat to the sheaf and has fulfilled his mystery". "You keep on talking of mystery," says his interlocutor (the raw youth). "What does it mean 'having fulfilled his mystery'?" Makar answers:

> "What is mystery? Everything is a mystery, dear; in all is God's mystery. In every tree, in

every blade of grass that same mystery lies hid.
Whether the tiny bird of the air is singing, or the
stars in all their multitudes shine at night in
heaven, the mystery is one, ever the same. And
the greatest mystery of all is what awaits the soul
of man in the world beyond. So it is, dear."

Up till now we have considered transcendence and
immanence in metaphors of space. But they can also
be stated in metaphors of time. Much Protestant
biblical theology uses metaphors of time to speak of
transcendence and immanence, but appears not to
realize that a metaphor is being used at all. So we
are teased out of thought by notions of the end of
the world having already occurred in advance in
Christ's resurrection. It is difficult for us to give
much meaning to such an idea, since a statement
has meaning only if it expresses a lived experience, and we have no experience of the end of the
world, since for us time and history continue to
march on. Blake put it better when he said that
eternity is in love with the productions of time. The
eternal God is always within the temporal process—
that is the mystery of time. He is, for instance,
present in the moral demands inherent in all situations, individual and communal. There is always
something we ought or ought not to do both as
individuals and as collectivities. That "ought" is the
mystery of the eternal in time. God is present in
judgement when selfishness and pride bring their
own horrific consequences on men and nations. And

He is present as our deliverer by wooing us away from thraldom to our fantasies, individual and communal, and drawing us towards the clear hard light of reality.

Most mysterious of all. He is present in all the pain and suffering of the world, not looking down upon it with Olympian detachment or benevolent concern, but Himself immersed in it up to the hilt. "In all our affliction, he was afflicted." The cross of Christ is the sign to us that wherever nature is red in tooth and claw and wherever men have to endure their agonies of bloody sweat or are the victims of oppression, injustice, or violence, there God is. And where God is, there Heaven is.

It is Dostoevsky again who has given us a most deeply moving picture of the truth here, this time in the person of Sonia, who, living in St Petersburg, can support her drunken father, her half-crazed mother, her young brothers and sisters only on the wages of prostitution. She talks to a friend, a young man called Raskolnikov, about God. He asks mockingly: "And what does God do for you?" Sonia replies, whispering and looking down—"He does everything." As L. A. Zander has commented: "For city-living Sonia God does not reveal Himself through nature, but through the hopeless and incomprehensible tragedy of human destiny," so that she is among those who "know and see that everything exists in God and that God is manifested in everything."

Perhaps this section on the relation between God

above and God within, eternity and time, transcendence and immanence, should end on a more technically philosophical note. If so, we could not do better than quote Karl Jaspers:

"God's infinity does not face finiteness as other —for then it would be finite also. God is the complete infinity which includes everything finite instead of confronting it."

GOD IN THE LONG LITTLENESS OF LIFE AND IN LIFE'S MAGNIFICENCE AND WRETCHEDNESS

The Long Littleness

If God is within us and within everything around us, and eternity catches time up into itself, then our discovery of God requires of us no esoteric journey into some spiritual stratosphere. It is in the grit of earth that we find the glory of heaven. It is in our being robustly human that God enables us to share His own divine life.

The Spanish St Teresa once blamed a confessor for imposing upon a busy housewife long periods of prayer. The housewife, said St Teresa, should have been shown how it was in the performance of her household chores that she praised God and held communion with Him. For God was present in her work just as much as in any oratory, and indeed, for a woman of her responsibilities, even more so.

God is always present and waiting to be discovered now, in the present moment, precisely where we are and in what we are doing. That is what we mean when we say that we live in a sacramental universe. Unfortunately we tend to treat the sacrament of our daily life, broken as it is into dozens of small, uneven bits and pieces, as something which hinders us from finding God when in fact it is the very vehicle of His presence. It is as though we were to complain that the bread and wine at the Holy Communion were obstacles to our approach to God instead of the means to it. If, as they do, the bread and wine on the altar represent all we are and do and suffer, then they show us that all our life in its manifold and often petty detail can become God's real presence with us, that it is in the daily bread of our ordinary common experience that we can discern the radiant body of everlasting life. The many things we have to do, the hundred and one calls on our time and attention, don't get between ourselves and God. On the contrary they are to us in very truth His Body and His Blood.

This is accepted without much difficulty when for

the moment our world consists of people who need
our help—the tramp who needs a meal, the neigh-
bour in distress who needs a talk over several glasses
of whisky, or the shy person who needs to be given
confidence. We remember "Inasmuch as ye did it"
and recognize God's presence. And it is no less easy
when we ourselves are the people in need and others
minister to us. It is not hard to recognize God in
their sensitive generosity and to praise Him for what
He is giving us through them. Perhaps we remember "Inasmuch as ye did it" even more when we are
on the receiver's side of the counter. And what goes
for personal and individual dealings of this kind
goes equally of course for the public and political
campaigns in which we engage. To join in public
communal action to establish righteousness (which
means humanness) in some place where it is denied
is obviously to find God at work in His power and
wisdom.

Where, however, we invariably fail to recognize
God's presence is within those many occasions
which are not conventionally associated with active
compassion and charity. ("Conventionally" here
means formally recognized, not, needless to say,
unreal.) For people continually give themselves
without their (or anybody else) often realizing what
they are doing. Self-giving is not (thank God)
confined to what are technically acts of piety or
compassion. I arrive, for instance, at a party feeling
dismal and dead. And there in talk and chatter I
find myself mixed up with a lot of mutual giving

and taking. The result is that I slowly become alive and begin to enjoy myself. A great deal of what appears in itself to be trivial empty talk—"Ghastly weather, isn't it?" "Did you hear what happened to Johnnie when he took the dog out last night?" "Betty's had her hair dyed!"—is in fact the machinery of communion between persons, the sacrament, the outward and audible sign of fellowship (a fact which people who are always wholly serious can never understand). Perhaps at the party I drank quite a bit, but drink on its own depresses rather than enlivens me. What renewed me was the contact with others the drink helped to establish. It was my blindness of heart, my false idea of God, which prevented me from recognizing the true *locale* of the party—that it was Cana of Galilee and that it was Christ Himself who had for the time being changed the water of my existence into wine. If I were to recognize only the possibility of that miracle when I have to meet other people, I should most likely begin to find myself enjoying what at first sight looked like the most unpromising social occasion.

Work

And, of course (as St Teresa knew) people give themselves in their daily work, however unspectacular it may be, and in their giving, there God is. Later we shall have to notice how one of the major problems of our time is that many people's work simply does not provide them with anything like

adequate opportunity for self-giving and that that is
the root cause of industrial unrest. But for those of
us who do not spend our time by a conveyor belt
there is little to impede us from finding God's
presence in our work, except for our spiritual
obtuseness, which, by the way, is probably not our
fault. (Most of us, if not born blind, soon become so,
owing to God knows what combinations of circum-
stance.)

Nature

As well as work, we can find God in what is called
nature. Because people can be sentimental about
the natural world (especially animals) and gush
about it with unreal cheap feeling, there is often an
inhibition in us about speaking of God in nature.
But that in fact is even more perverse than the sentimentality, for the experience of God in nature has
always been widespread and strong. (We have only
to read the psalms to see that.) But it is to be feared
that many professional religionists like to keep God
within the confines of their professional capacities
(perhaps they fear being made redundant) and so
they tend to belittle the God who inhabits the hills,
whose glory can also be found in a dog, and point
people to Church and Bible as the places where the
real God can alone be found with adequate guarantees. It is understandable but again perverse, since
the Bible itself, and not least the teaching and par-
ables of Jesus, is full of references to God's

presence in the natural world. It is God, said Jesus, who clothes the grass of the field and the lilies as they grow and it is He who feeds the birds of the air, while there is a special providence in the fall of a sparrow.

What of God we discover in Nature depends upon our needs and our capacity to receive what is offered. The fact that in the Far East there is the green hell of endless forest in no way legitimizes our sneering at those who see God in the beauty and splendour of the natural world, nor does it excuse our speaking superciliously of Wordsworth in the tropics. It is only in terms of our actual situation that we can see and perceive, not in terms of a hypothetical one—and we do not live in the tropics. Perhaps if we did, the green hell would speak to us of that terrifying and relentless power of God of which Job was allowed to become aware. (It is an intriguing but profitless speculation—Wordsworth into Job, though Wordsworth certainly had his first intimations of what was devastatingly revealed to Job.) It is the signs of God's presence in the nature we know that we need to be concerned about.

They must be as many and various as people are. What is of particular interest to some is the unity in the natural world of its scientific and aesthetic interest. Scientists are interested in the mechanics whereby the natural world goes about its business. Artists are interested in its colours, its light and shade, its shapes and proportions. Yet the world of the scientist and artist is one, for nature "in the very act of

labouring like a machine, also sleeps like a picture.
. . . The machinery is itself the painting, the useful laws compose the spectacle". Of this Simone Weil has given a particular example: "In the beauty of the world rude necessity becomes an object of love. What is more beautiful than the action of weight on the fugitive waves of the sea, or the almost eternal folds of the mountains?"

Learned men (as St Teresa of Avila invariably calls theologians, sincerely, but with just the faintest hint of mockery) tell us that in God being and activity are one, that God is what He does and does what He is. If so, nature labouring like a machine while it sleeps like a picture is very much a revelation of God. And where God reveals Himself, there He is.

Art

God reveals Himself also in art of all kinds—written, visual, audible. For art, when true to itself, attempts to bring into the sharpest possible focus some aspect or other of reality, how it threatens and ennobles, destroys and creates, its tragedies and triumphs, thus waking us up from our comforting dreams and consoling illusions—or maybe from our nightmares.

So, for instance, Judge Brack at the end of *Hedda Gabler* points to our own blindness when he says: "People don't behave like that," because the play has just shown that in fact they do. On the other

side there is the story of Charles Gore, encountered
one evening "in the corridor of the Queen's Hall
after the orchestra had played a Brandenburg con-
certo. His almost unconscious comment on the
music showed where it had led his thoughts: 'If *that*
is true, everything must be all right.'"

Wherever reality of any kind is revealed, there
God must be. For it is only in His light that we can
see light, which means also that it is only in His
light that we can perceive darkness.

Ourselves

If only in a weak and derivative sense, we are all of
us artists in that we all have to produce set-pieces—
work out plans, make arrangements, solve problems, see to it that things are or will be in order.
This means that we have to think things over quite
a lot, and we shall probably find ourselves thinking
them over when (we feel) we should be attending to
other things. Of course there is unnecessary worry
and flap and obviously we must try to keep a sense
of proportion. But that agreed, when we are thinking things out to solve a problem or set something in
order, it is the Creator Spirit Himself at work in us,
energizing within the limits and quirks of our
human condition, creating the answer by enabling
us in our fumbling way to work it out for ourselves.

When, for instance, somebody is writing a book,
he may often find it almost impossible to pray in the
ordinary sense of being still and receptive in the

presence of God, since he cannot help thinking about what he is going to write, whether in what he has already written he has in some place or other expressed himself badly or whether the whole plan of the book needs revising. In those circumstances he must not be misled into fighting against God. For it is God Himself, the Creator Spirit, who has set his mind fermenting in this untidy and distracting way.

An old priest who had devoted his life to the people of the East End of London used (as old men often do) to speak his thoughts out loud. To hear him celebrate the Holy Communion made Christianity live for you in laughter and tears. For throughout the service he would proceed thus: "Let us pray for the whole state of Christ's Church militant here in earth. I must remember to see about those turkeys for the old people's Christmas dinner." "Make your humble confession to Almighty God meekly kneeling upon your knees. Perhaps I'd better call again on those damned electricians. They never come when they say they will." He was near enough to God not to be worried by these disturbances from the Creator Spirit.

Sex

But perhaps more important than anything is that we should recognize God in our sexual feelings.

Our concern here is not with the morality of sexual behaviour, its rights and wrongs, though rights and wrongs it certainly has. Our concern here is simply with the feelings of sexual attraction.

God is present in those feelings in order that we may care for, be concerned about, be patient and take trouble with the people who sexually attract us. Doubtless it is our duty to be all these things to everybody coming within our ken, a duty that we should perform as conscientiously as possible. But if it is only a matter of duty the performance will lack wings, however hard we try. Those who do good by effort are certainly praiseworthy, but they do not always show goodness to the best advantage. Their goodness "is apt to betray too much in them the machinery of its growth and will be in some degree formal and artificial in tone". Then let us thank God for our sexual feelings, for in them He is turning duty into pleasure so that we may be really in rapport with the people who attract us, even though we may be innocently unaware of the nature of the attraction, since our sexual feelings include a rag-bag which few of us think of scrutinizing too closely or indeed dare to. And we must remember that pleasure requires its own wisdom and self-control, its own asceticism if it is not to turn sour. "God is powerful", said the late Father P. N. Waggett of Cowley, "on both sides of every pressure."

But the tragic thing is that somewhere deep in our unconscious there lies the fantasy of God as the jealous rival of what sexually attracts us instead of His being, as He is, its creator. Hence the fantastic overestimation of virginity in the Catholic tradition of Christianity. Until only a few years ago in one of

the services to be said on the feast of the Holy
Innocents, those slaughtered infants were eulogized
with the words: "These are they who have not
defiled themselves with women: for they are virgins.
Alleluia."

A more English version of God disapproving of
sexual feeling was provided (in sad parody) by
Studdert Kennedy:

> "Pray! Have I prayed—when I've bored the
>   saints with praying,
>   When I've stunned the blessed angels with my
>   battery of prayer,
>   —When I've used the time in saying—but it's
>   only saying, saying,
>   —And I cannot get to Jesus for the Glory of her
>   hair."

On this Geoffrey Beaumont commented: "Studdert
Kennedy knew as well as you and I that in reality it
is through the glory of her hair that we come to
God, that there we would find Jesus if we would
only recognize Him."

Blindness is the parent of hypocrisy—"Thou
blind pharisee" as Jesus said. There is something
nauseatingly hypocritical in Christians holding up
their hands in pious horror at the excesses of what is
called the permissive society, when they themselves
down the ages have tried so hard and so persistently
to keep God out of sex. It is a harvest of their own
sowing that they are now reaping, and the hell they
abhor is in large part a hell of their own lighting up.

MYSTERY AGAIN: ALL DESCRIBED AS NOTHING

We have spoken of finding God within and around us. It may therefore be necessary to repeat what was said briefly in a former section about God not being a definable entity. Discovering God, we said, meant sensing the presence of mystery.

We shall not find God anywhere if we equate Him with some spiritual personage about whom we picked up information in childhood or adolescence ("Do not be children in your thinking," said St Paul, "be babes in evil, but in thinking be mature.") —an object out there who, if not exactly an old man, may be (as he was for Mr Polly) a kind of schoolmaster with unlimited powers of espial, or perhaps an ethereal kind of electricity or an oblong blur. If we equate God with that sort of picture or preconception, then, as Tillich used to say, the atheist is right; there is no God.

Who, however, can avoid discovering mystery?

By the word mystery here is meant not a problem as yet unsolved, which in principle could be solved and may well be so as research pushes back the frontiers of knowledge, but an experience so profound that it must always beggar our processes of thinking, of cerebration, because it eludes classification and analysis and breaks through the walls of categorization. Shakespeare described a mystery of this kind in *The Phoenix and the Turtle*:

> "Reason in itself confounded
> Saw division grow together;
> To themselves yet either neither,
> Simple were so well compounded.

> "That it cried, 'How true a twain
> Seemeth this concordant one!
> Love has reason, reason none,
> If what parts can so remain.'"

There are, for instance, biological and psychological elements in human love, and these can be investigated and described in what nowadays is regrettably called an on-going process. We may hope to know more about them in a hundred years' time than we do now. But human love at its deepest, most satisfying and most sacrificial transcends (while it does not exclude) any possible descriptions of its biological and psychological dynamics. Ultimately it is a mystery. Or some overpowering sense of compassion that tells us (as it told the Good Samaritan) that we *must* go to the help of a person in need—that sense of compassion cannot be reduced to any sum of rational or utilitarian calculations. That, too, is a mystery.

If, as Christians, we are not to deny goodness when we see it (something which approaches very

near to the sin against the Holy Ghost), then we
have to admit that many people believe in God and
truly serve Him even if it be under formulas that
appear to deny Him. And this will still be so however much they may protest against our conclusion.
"The implicit adherence to a truth", said Simone
Weil, "can in some cases be worth as much as the
explicit adherence, sometimes a great deal more."
So people who find depth in some of the occasions of
life and sense there the presence of mystery (parents, for instance, invariably do when their first
child is born) are finding God there. The love of
naturalists for what they observe is very hard to
distinguish from worship, even though they may
think themselves agnostics or atheists, while the
atmosphere at a Promenade Concert at the Albert
Hall is like a religious service, or rather, like what a
religious service should be, with the audience silent,
attentive, expectant of good things, and then gloriously grateful and enthusiastic when these have
been received.

Two Sorts of Person

The truth that God is mystery needs stressing for
two sorts of person. The first are those who think
they know with some precision who or what God is
like. It is they who need Eckhart's reminder that
"he who seeks God under settled form lays hold on
the form while missing the God concealed in it".
The others are those who stumble at all and every

form, and who therefore conclude either that there is no God or that, if there is a Something Somewhere Somehow, it is too remote and vague a reality for communion with it to be possible. Man tends, said Coleridge, either "to lose the ONE in striving after the INFINITE [i.e. Atheism] or the INFINITE in striving after the ONE [i.e., anthropomorphic monotheism]"—God as some exalted kind of human figure. But the truly religious person will say with George Macdonald:

> "I see thy light, I feel thy wind,
>   The world, it is thy word,
>   Whatever wakes my heart and mind,
>   Thy presence is, my Lord."

So if it is God alone who can fill the hole in the human heart, He can do it without people having to accept this or the other conceptualization of Him, or indeed any conceptualization at all. As Rabbi Abraham Herschel has said: "Transcendence can never be an object of possession or comprehension. Yet man can relate himself and be engaged to it." And was it not St John of the Cross who finally discovered that it was only by the word Nada that he could express his experience of Todo, that in the end it was only the word Nothing which could describe the All?

JOY IS KNOWING

So far joy has been considered as a feeling, a more or less vivid emotion of delight and gladness. That is natural. For when we think of joy it is a feeling of that sort which first comes to mind.

Perhaps, however, the matter needs probing a bit further. We could, for instance, ask whether feeling is in fact the primary or fundamental reality of joy, however vital the inclusion of feeling may be in any adequately rounded description of it. A lover will say of his beloved that she is his joy as a mother will say of her child or a connoisseur of his pictures. What they are referring to as their joy is the source from which their feelings spring. And the source of something is prior, both in logic and in life, to what springs from it, as cause is prior to effect. Indeed in the situations just described (if we were allowed a rather loose use of language) we could envisage the cause existing without the effect, the source of joy without its evoking any corresponding feeling. The young woman would still be immensely attractive and lovable even if her suitor's feeling for her had diminished to zero. The child would still be a precious being of infinite worth even if its unnatural mother had ceased to care for it at all. While the pictures, supposing them to have been inherited by a Philistine with no glimmer of aesthetic sensibility, would still be the masterpieces they always were.

To be sure, those are no more than inadequate images of the joy we were created to discover and appropriate, the Joy of God which alone can finally satisfy us. But they do indicate certain important things about it that can be easily overlooked.

To begin with, when we speak of the Joy of God we do not speak of it, at least in its primary sense, as we might speak of the joy of stamp collecting. For in stamp collecting the joy inheres entirely in the collector. If collecting stamps brings him no joy, then joy does not exist, since the stamps in themselves have no value at all except as a financial investment which might just as well be in sausages or sugar. When, however, we speak of the Joy of God we do not in the first instance refer to any feelings of joy that may be communicated to us. We refer to God Himself in His own eternal life. For His eternal life is Joy.

The doctrine of the Trinity is unsatisfying, even ridiculous, when attempts are made to define it too closely. But considered as an image of God as Joy it comes into its own. For there can be no joy where there is no communication with otherness. (Self-enclosed isolation is the reverse of joyous.) Further, this communion with otherness can become so close that it is indistinguishable from identity—the fact which Shakespeare so fantastically described in *The Phoenix and the Turtle*. It is a state which is at least approached when two people love each other deeply and maturely. In such close communion otherness is transcended, but it is not abolished. Other-

wise joy could not be full. To speak of God as
Trinity, with otherness and identity combined
(however as a matter of history the doctrine arose)
is to use an image for Him which underlines His
eternal Being as vibrant and inexhaustible Joy.

Primarily, therefore, the Joy of God is simply
God Himself, what He eternally is. It is a Joy which
consists of responsiveness to otherness, a responsiveness which issues in self-giving to otherness and
is completed when the other in its turn shows a
corresponding responsiveness and self-giving. Such
is the mystery of God Three in One who is Joy.

Allowing ourselves once again a rather loose use
of words we might say that it is the nature of joy
when full to overflow. Such at least has been the
Christian understanding of God's continuous creation of the universe. The universe is the overflowing
of God's Joy, the calling into existence of further
otherness to which in Joy God gives Himself so that
in Joy it may correspondingly give itself to Him.
And if this Joy includes, as we know it does, suffering and death, that at least bears witness to the fact
that the Joy of *being* infinitely exceeds the satisfac-
tions of *having*, even of having physical life itself. In
the death and resurrection of Christ, Christians see
proclaimed this triumph of being over having, being
which is Joy because it is responsiveness to the
Other and self-giving to that Other to the utter-
most.

If in the first instance the Joy of God is God
Himself, then in a secondary sense the Joy of God is

God's gift of the Joy which is Himself both to us and
to His whole creation.

As far as we are concerned, this gift of Himself, of
Joy, will certainly find expression in our feelings,
but not in any superficial way. The Joy of God is
not spiritual bubbly (though that may occasionally
be one of its least important by-products). It does
not consist in what is called feeling good—"My
dear, I'm having the most divine time," as Ruth
Draper's débutante used to say. When God gives us
His Joy, that is when He Himself comes to us and
makes His abode with us, He abides at the very
deepest level of what we are, indeed at so deep a
level that His presence does not always surface to
conscious awareness, at least of any strong kind
(although it may sometimes do that like the burning
newspaper used to begin lighting a fire). God's Joy
in us is more like one of those characters in a novel
or play who enter the scene shy, silent, and self-
effacing, but who gradually assert their ascendancy
without any of the other characters realizing what is
going on, until they suddenly discover that the shy
young girl, or whoever it is, is in complete control.
It is this gradual and unrecognized growth of God's
Joy within us which is the important thing.
Whether or not we have emotional spasms thrilling
us through is of little significance. In any case such
spasms are often little more than a hotch-potch of
superficial but unassimilated and unorientated feelings finding at last an outlet—something in itself
entirely legitimate and indeed God-given, so long as

we do not overvalue it, as though we thought that
our being stirred by one of Sousa's marches was
identical with a person's being caught up in one of
Beethoven's quartets.

As God's Joy grows within us it enables us to
perceive His Joy in the world around us. And just as
within ourselves God's Joy is often hidden like the
mustard seed in the earth, so, too, around us it will
often be hidden under this or another disguise.
God's Joy within us will slowly enable us to see
through the disguise to the reality; or perhaps better
put, it will enable us to discern in the apparent
disguise the very stuff and material in which God is
present and at work. That can happen when we
observe the apparently trivial: "The importance of
the novelist's art in its highest form", said Gabriel
Marcel, "is that it shows us that the insignificant,
strictly speaking, cannot and does not exist." It can
happen when we see the potentialities for good
inherent in what shows itself as its contrary; con-
traries like pride of possession, love of money, the
search for power or prestige, and sexual promi-
scuity—for in all these things people are blindly
seeking after God, rather like a wasp which is trying
to get into the open air will often do no more than
persistently dash itself against a pane of glass. And
most of all we discern God's Joy at work when we
come across suffering—in others or ourselves. In all
the Joy of God lies waiting with infinite patience for
its appointed time, working continually on every
kind of recalcitrant raw material until it can deliver

as golden what formerly was brazen. And (as we saw) we can perceive God's Joy thus secretly at work in those around us because that same Joy is also at work within us.

But that means that the Joy of God is a cognitive faculty. It is a way of seeing and knowing. It gives us both eyes and understanding. It opens up the world to us—not only the world of other people but (as we have tried to show) the world of nature and of art.

God's Joy as a way of knowing will of course have its repercussions on our feelings. But it is an infinitely deeper thing, and infinitely more real, than what we usually mean by the word "feelings". For it is the most real of all realities, God Himself—God Himself with us and with all things.

TWO WAYS OF KNOWING: OUTSIDERS AND INSIDERS

But we must now ask: How do we know all this?

The shortest answer is that given by Coleridge: "In the same way exactly that you know that your eyes were made to see with; that is, because you *do* see with them." In Joy we *do* perceive the presence of joy in all things and that should assure us that

God's Joy within us is a true and valid way of seeing and knowing.

Of course it might all be a mirage, a projection, a form of wish-fulfilment. That logical possibility can never be excluded just as the chairs and tables may exist only in our minds without possessing any external actuality. Such Absolute Idealism (in the technical philosophical sense) can never be finally disproved. But we trust the evidences of our senses none the less and believe that the chairs and tables are actually there in the external world. And no greater act of faith is required to trust the evidence of our spiritual sensibilities. But that granted, the question "How do we know?" still needs answering.

It looks as if men perceive and know in two main ways, which may be described as a higher and a lower way. The higher way is the power of intuitively apprehending reality—what the medieval schoolmen called *intellectus* and which, following their example, we shall call *Intelligence*. It is very near, if not identical, with what in the Old Testament and Apocrypha is called Wisdom: "Happy is the man who finds wisdom and the man who gets understanding", for "she is a tree of life to those who lay hold of her", since "the Lord by wisdom founded the earth, and by his understanding he established the heavens." Wisdom "in every generation passes into holy souls and makes them friends of God", and "whoever loves wisdom loves life, and those who seek her early will be filled with joy". The lower way of knowing is the capacity for

putting two and two together and coming to a
logical conclusion—what the schoolmen called *ratio*
(we generally think of it as brain-power) and which
we shall call *Deliberation*.

These two do not conflict with each other or need
not. They should be complementary. Our intuitive
apprehension (what we are calling Intelligence)
provides the material for our brain-power (what we
are calling Deliberation) to work upon as we put
two and two together.

Intelligence (in the special sense in which we are
using the word) is by no means identical with what
we normally call our intellect. For the intellect
merely inspects things from the outside, adds up the
details provided by the inspection and comes to a
conclusion—and that is the function performed by
the mechanism we have called Deliberation. Intelligence, on the other hand, does not inspect its
object from the outside. It enters into its object,
delves deep down into its object's innermost reality,
clothes itself with its object, puts on its object as part
of itself, and hence in the end abolishes the distinction between itself as perceiving subject and the
other as object perceived. In this sense Intelligence
realizes its object, takes it up as part of its own identity. Two people who love each other deeply can do
this. Their knowledge of each other is the knowledge of Intelligence and passes infinitely beyond
the knowledge of Deliberation. They live in each
other. In the biblical image, they are one flesh. But
the knowledge of Intelligence is not confined to

people who deeply love each other, even if it is most apparent there. It can extend to all people and to things. A man can love his cronies in the pub in the sense that he knows them with the intuitive knowledge of Intelligence and in some degree they live in him as he does in them, so that if one of them dies, the death of the crony is felt in part as his own death. A man can also love the hills where he walks, the pictures in the gallery he goes to see, the house he has long lived in. Here too we have examples of the knowledge of Intelligence, for in some way or other the man has taken them up into himself as a living part of what he is. His personal identity is not outside what he knows, but includes it.

Many people have tried in many ways to describe the way of knowing we have called Intelligence. D. H. Lawrence, for instance, wrote of the two ways of knowing for man and contrasted "knowing in terms of apartness which is mental, rational, scientific" (what we have called Deliberation), and "knowing in terms of togetherness which is religious and poetic". And he left no doubt that he thought the second had a purchase upon reality while the first destroyed it. The young Coleridge (he was only twenty-two) in a letter to Southey shows himself, by the use of a vivid image, finding his way to the same conclusion. He writes of the act of knowing a truth as swallowing it and continues:

"It is not enough that we have once swallowed it—The *Heart* should have *fed* upon the *truth*, as

Insects on a leaf—till it be tinged with the colour,
and shew its food in every the minutest fibre."

D. H. Lawrence's emphasis on knowledge in terms
of togetherness combines two kinds of togetherness.
What is referred to is not only the togetherness of
the knower and the object known (like the insect
being tinged with the colour of the leaf it feeds on)
but also the togetherness of the human knower; that
is to say, he knows with his guts as well as with his
mind, with his unconscious as well as with his conscious self. Deliberation is a lower way of knowing
than Intelligence because, among other things, it
uses only the mind and not the guts, only the conscious and not the unconscious self. It involves only
a small part of what a person is, not the whole of it.

> "God guard me from those thoughts men think
>   In the mind alone;
>   He that sings a lasting song
>   Thinks in a marrow bone."

When I know by the way of Intelligence, everything I am is included in my act of knowing: guts,
mind, heart, body, as when a man (in the biblical as
in all other senses) knows his wife.

The way we know the Joy of God is by knowing
in terms of togetherness, by what we have called the
way of Intelligence. We know the Joy of God by
entering into it, putting it on, *realizing* it, so that it
becomes part of our own identity. Yet these images
of entering and putting on can be misleading

because they suggest that God's Joy is something we have to go out and acquire when in fact it is already within us and always has been, although it may be in a deep sleep and need awakening.

When the Joy of God is thus asleep in us the whole world (including ourselves) seems weary, stale, flat and unprofitable. We are alone with our own damned selves, "the noise of passions ringing us for dead unto a place where is no rest". Other people are a bore when they are not a torture. Our work seems a form of persecution. We are out of tune with the arts. The natural world seems empty and dead.

But to the degree in which the Joy of God is awoken within us, to that degree it recognizes the Joy of God in the world, going out to meet it and claiming it as its own. In the words of the fourth-century morning hymn:

> "Earth's gloom flees broken and dispersed
> By the sun's piercing shafts coerced;
> The day-star's eyes rain influence bright,
> And colours glimmer back to sight."

When Christians speak of the mystery of their redemption it is to this awakening of God's Joy in the heart that they are at least partly referring. And in so far as they assert that this redemption has an objective side to it, are they not asserting that God's Joy can be awoken in a heart without the person concerned thinking of it in those terms at all? Perhaps all he will think is that he has found himself

or found life. But none the less it is the Joy of God
he will have found. A duchess who was the Queen's
Mistress of the Robes said that at a fête she was
once identified by somebody as "the lady who
took the sugar without the tongs". Maybe our
orthodox identifications of God are as funny as that,
almost certainly much funnier.

In whatever terms we conceptualize or think
about it, once it is awoken, God's Joy within us
recognizes His Joy around us. It is God's Joy which
is with the scientist as he pursues his researches,
with the artist in the exercise of his craft, with the
administrator as he brings order out of muddle,
with parents as they nurture their children, with
friends as they gossip and children as they play
together. Any life worth living is the Joy of God in
us going out to meet His Joy in the world—the Joy
we come to know by the way of Intelligence (for
God works by means of our faculties, not in spite of
them), as we intuitively apprehend God's Joy and
realize it as our own. As de Caussade puts it:

> "It is for God, who gives life to all things, to
> revive the soul with regard to His creation and to
> give a different [i.e. not neutral or dead] aspect to
> all things in the eyes of the soul. It is the com-
> mand of God which is this life. By this command
> the heart goes out to the created world . . . and it
> is also by this command that the created world is
> carried towards the soul and accepted by it", so
> that in consequence "each moment contains all."

It is, as we have said more than once, in the world
of nature that many people find the Joy of God most
transparently present. And in this connection the
words of Simone Weil are relevant:

> "The beauty of the world is not an attribute of
> matter in itself. It is a relationship of the world to
> our sensibility, the sensibility which depends
> upon the structure of our body and our soul. . . .
> The beauty of the world is Christ's tender smile
> for us coming through matter. The love of this
> beauty proceeds from God dwelling in our souls
> and goes out to God present in the universe. It is
> like a sacrament."

St Paul once said that all things are ours. We are
now in the position to understand how. All things
are not ours by way of possession. Indeed it would
be intolerable if they were. For the tragedy of even
great possessions is that most of them cannot be as-
similated by their possessor, who remains outside
them as an alien. That is why multi-millionaires
sometimes go and hide themselves in an hotel suite.
All things are ours, not by way of possession, but by
the recognition in them of the Joy which is also
ours—and God's. That is why St Francis of Assisi
called everything Sister This or Brother That. It
wasn't sentimentality. It was his perception in them
of the Joy by which he himself had been overcome.

THE TRICKY CUSTOMER AGAIN—HIS REAL FALSE IDENTITY

But for those of us ordinary mortals who are not a St Francis, Joy still remains very largely the tricky customer we encountered at the outset, capricious and elusive. We are now, however, in a better position than we were to understand why.

At the outset we thought that it was Joy itself which was the tricky customer—the feelings on which our hold was so tenuous and which were always saying good-bye. But now we have seen that Joy can be spelt with a capital letter because Joy is its source which is God, the God who is the most real of all realities and who in His eternal being and activity never changes. If therefore joy (ordinary, everyday, human-centred joy) still appears to us as a tricky customer, no better than a faithless and inconstant lover, we can now see that the tricky customer is a projection (like a cloud) of ourselves upon Joy, the Joy which in fact is ever actively the same and for which in our bones we know that we were made.

Why are we tricky customers?

Because each of us tends to equate what he is
with only a small fraction of his full self. This makes
us imagine that we are no more than self-enclosed
conscious egos whose relation to others, to the world
and even to God is that of us here and them over
there—what could be called a relationship of exter-
nality. We imagine that each of us is an individual
unit, ultimately isolated, but a unit which has at
least the advantage that it can think, i.e., put two
and two together. The individual isolated unit in its
cut-offness supposes that the best use it can make of
its ability to put two and two together is in the
service of its self-defence. And in order thus to
defend itself the individual unit, the self-enclosed
conscious ego, becomes acquisitive, attempting all
the time to snatch from its world materials out of
which to build an empire—materials like wealth,
prestige, recognition, regard, religiosity, what it
considers sexual success or even what it considers to
be love—all the things, in fact (including the
religiosity), which are the objects of what is technically known as concupiscence; thus stuffing the
ego-self with goodies in order that it may the more
effectively ward off any attacks that may be made
upon it. In consequence the ego-self feels that it is
under a continued threat of loss and that therefore it
must keep a wary eye upon its empire lest one or
other of its outposts be taken from it. With the ego-
self thus under perpetual siege, it is no wonder that
joy appears such a tricky customer. We have, after
all, so little time left for it. "How hardly shall they

that have riches enter into the kingdom of God,"
said Jesus.

Simplification often makes a point clearer. So for
this purpose let us tell a silly story, even if it takes
simplification into the borders of the ridiculous:

John, George, Mary and Sue were four young
people who went out together for a picnic. The
weather was perfect and the country ravishing.
They should have enjoyed themselves immensely.
But each of them had equated what he or she was
with a false self, which was but a tiny fraction of his
or her true self. John was a clever journalist who
thought he would disappear unless he were continually trying to be clever. George was by way of
being a tennis star who had recently arrived at the
lower reaches of Wimbledon and in everything he
said he pointed, however indirectly and obliquely,
to his successes on the tennis court. Mary was a social
worker (she came from an affluent family) who
identified herself entirely with what she liked to call
her social conscience and felt that its somewhat con-
demnatory deliverances were her only claim to attention. Sue was a professional beauty (unkind
people called her a suburban belle) who sat most of
the time like a statue as if daring people not to see
how superbly beautiful she was. The picnic which
promised so well turned out to be a misery. How
could it fail to? Each member of the party spent all
the time on the defensive, protecting that one aspect
of themselves with which they had identified the

whole. Joy had no need to say good-bye because it had never been present. It had been excluded from the start by the anxiety of all concerned to guard their possessions. Yet all four of them were in themselves, apart from their special line, attractive and lovable people. But they couldn't believe it.

It is only to the degree in which this artificially fabricated ego is broken down that we can find Joy. It is only by thus dying that we can begin to live. We have, all of us, only two options before us: lust or life. And by lust is not meant exclusively, or even chiefly, sexual lust. (There is an irony which would be terrible were it not amusing when do-gooders are loud in their condemnations of sexual lust while they themselves are very much more lustful when it is a matter of power or reputation. They are like individuals who are three-quarters blind and who say of the people in front of them: "I see clearly that these people have shockingly defective eyesight." Lust means ego empire-building, enlarging, and at all costs protecting, the false fabricated self. And it can take not only the most respectable but also the most ascetic and apparently religious forms. And always it is a prescription for misery. And the joke is that it doesn't really please even the false self. For this ramshackle empire is in the final resort too anxious to find Joy. Rimbaud put it with his customarily brutal honesty: "Like a wild beast I pounced blindly on every joy that I might throttle it," though, unlike Rimbaud, when we throttle Joy we keep up the appearances of civilization and indeed often imagine that it is civilization itself we are helping to preserve.

Our predicament is that we are half-in-half people, partly fabricated false selves and partly people who have discovered their true identity in openness to others, whatever the risks involved, and in active exhilarating communion with God and with all things in Him—which is the quintessence of Joy. It is thus as half-in-halfers that we are caught in the limitation between un-being and being, since we are both citizens of Heaven on earth and also self-excluded exiles from it.

But God, because He is our Saviour, does not leave the false fabricated self to rest in peace. He continually disturbs it. When Ralph Waldo Emerson wrote: "People wish to be settled; only in so far as they are unsettled is there any hope for them," his words could not have better described the action of God's saving power within us. God's disturbance of us can take every sort of form and degree, and it will be mediated to us by means of our circumstances and disposition.

The disturbance may be violent, as in breakdown or in some radical alteration (we think for the worse) in our customary manner of life. It may come as anger towards (as we suppose) the writer of a book with whose opinions we disagree. It could come as the collapse of long-cherished and strenuously worked-for plans for a son or daughter. It could be the social revolution which is disrupting our place in society. Or it could be no more than an ache in the background of what we are, more evident at some times than at others, an ache of frustration or discontent. "Time's violence", it has been said, "rends the soul; by the rent eternity enters." When life hits us, either strenuously with a big blow or by the constant nagging of petty annoyance (to which the smothered unrest deep within us makes us prone), we should pray to recognize it for what it is—the hand upon us of the God who is our Saviour breaking up the false fabricated self. He seldom does it all at once. His demolition work is generally carried on by stages, pulling down first this bit and then that.

The slow death of the false self, the self-enclosed ego, is not pleasant for anybody. It is bound to be a matter of misery and pain for all on whom it falls.

But it comes with a special poignancy on people who are religious and who sincerely believe that they have really been trying (as indeed they have) to love God. For mixed up with their genuine outgoing love for God there has been an attempt, without their being aware of it, to use God as an ally of their self-enclosed egos, the protector of the religious empire they have so carefully built up within them. And they have confused this self-made religious empire with God Himself. So when God, by means of this or that, begins to break up this false religious ego-self, the devout often tend at first to be angry with the people they choose to cast as the destroyers of their faith. And then, if the process of demolition goes on, they feel left without any divine support in a state of what they imagine is total unbelief. But what in fact they have ceased to believe in is their own idea of God as the buttress of their own religious egos, and it is God who has smashed up their ideas of Himself in order to destroy their false fabricated religious identities.

Alan Ecclestone has recently reminded us that this divine demolition work is precisely what our religious devotions are intended to bring about. "To 'use' a sacrament", he says, "is to expose ourselves to the winds of change, to evince a willingness to be disturbed within and without by pressures we may not like." And in his support he could have quoted his beloved Charles Péguy: "A great philosophy is not one which goes unchallenged. . . . It is one which has something to say even if it does not manage to say it. . . . A great philosopher is not one . . . who establishes a definitive truth; a philosopher is a man who introduces anxiety." For it is by anxiety that God often begins to break up the isolated ego in its religious no less than in its other aspects.

We can often see the truth most calmly and therefore most clearly in past history, since what is past can no longer threaten us. A letter from Bishop Stubbs of Oxford to Charles Gore, the recent contributor to and editor of *Lux Mundi* (published in 1889), is here, therefore, of interest. Gore had championed the kind of biblical criticism that is now taken for granted by almost all Christians and without which

Christianity would not have survived in the modern world except among a lunatic fringe. Stubbs wrote:

> "I do not think that you are at all aware of the terrible effect your teaching is having, on these points [i.e. the critical approach to the Bible], among faithful people. . . . Even if you choose to look on me as a Philistine or a Foolometer, you will I think see how other Philistines etc., are likely to regard both the teaching and the wanton way in which it is being spread. You make me anxious enough I can tell you."

It is important for us to discover what, in the last quarter of the twentieth century, is the equivalent for Christian belief of the challenge brought by biblical criticism in the last quarter of the nineteenth century.

THE TRUE SELF

When, however, God destroys the false self with its false securities, He does so to make room for the true self to grow. There will probably be a time-lag between our awareness of the destruction and our awareness of what is growing, but the growth in fact begins at the very moment of demolition; or rather, the dying of this or that aspect of the false self is always a sign that we are ready to receive from God what we truly are. And the more we receive from God what we truly are, the more content shall we be for the ramshackle empire of our isolated ego to collapse. Of course it doesn't happen in a day. It is a long, costly—and glorious—process.

The self we truly are, the self which flows directly from God's continuous creative act, is a self alive with an inexpressibly rich quality of life because it is totally open (and hence totally vulnerable) to its own inner dispositions (none of which it disavows), to other people, to the truth wherever it may lead, to the created world in its profusion and variety sometimes threatening and sometimes succouring us, to pleasure—and to affliction. And in all these things it finds the God who is Joy. It is a self that knows in the deepest places of its being that nothing can separate it from the love of God, and that His love, spread abroad and, so to speak, solidified in His world, is Joy unspeakable and full of glory. It is a self that confronts the recurrent "in spite of" of human living (in spite of my misfortune or illness or of Betty's death) and swallows up this "in spite of" with the triumphant "how much more" of God's self-giving love. For God makes of a loss that is real and devastating the means of an increased apprehension of Himself, which is our only ultimate gain—though that is a truth that it may take years or a lifetime to realize.

What we have described has well been called the

logic of superabundance. That logic of superabundance, of God's continuous and increasing gift of Himself to us, is the context in which the true self breathes and lives. Concupiscence, clutching at things (including God), is entirely absent because we can lose nothing without gaining more.

THE ATTRACTIVE LOVER

God leads us to find our true self in Him by His attractiveness. He lures us like the lover He is. If we are unaware of His attractiveness, it is because we are too preoccupied to notice it. In this respect we are like visitors touring a stately home who fail to take much, if any, notice of the masterpiece by Rembrandt hanging on the wall, so preoccupied are they with getting to the old stables where lunches are served. God's attractiveness is attested to by everybody who takes the trouble to be regularly still and silent in His presence attending to Him— though at the start we shall probably need the help of an experienced guide. One of the most promising features of our time is that more and more people are discovering that they *want* to meditate or contemplate or whatever they call it, not because it brings any calculable result but because of its own inherent value. They are discovering God's attractiveness and in so doing are discovering their own true selves.

Art

God's attractiveness is also experienced when it is (as we said) solidified in His world. In a previous section we have already noticed the testimony borne by art to reality. Here we are concerned with its power to attract. So compelling can be the attractive power of a work of art that it can deliver us, for the time being at least, from the vicious circle of our obsessions, making us, as we say, forget ourselves in the splendour of what we behold. As Iris Murdoch has said: "We are attracted to the real in the guise of the beautiful and the response to this attraction brings joy. . . . The proper apprehension of beauty is joy in reality through the transfiguring of desire. Thus as we respond we experience the transcendence of the real," and this vision of transcendent reality delivers us from anxiety about our (false) selves.

It is worth noticing here that it is not by what we earlier called Deliberation that we respond to a work of art (though that may be a preliminary— knowing about schools of painting, music, etc.), but by what we called Intelligence—the going out into the picture or music so that it becomes part of what we are and we discover there something of our true selves. The picture or music which attracts us and into whose being we enter is not, to be sure, in itself God. But it is the vehicle of His presence. For surely Flannery O'Connor is right when she says that the artist penetrates the concrete world in order to find at its depths the image of ultimate reality. Christians should not begrudge agnostics their experience of ultimacy (God) and its power to attract, nor deny that in this way they are discovering their true selves.

Other People

But if in thus being open to a work of art we discover something of what we truly are, that is commonly much more the case when we are open to other people.

This openness to others takes the form of a patient and profound listening to them, a concentrated attention to them that hears what they don't say even more than what they do say. It is perhaps the hardest work in which we ever engage, but it results in our discovery of their lovableness, hidden though it may sometimes be under successive layers of repellent distortion. And the lovableness we thus gradually discover goes deeper (although it is less obvious) than sexual attraction, though it does not exclude the sexual element, which, if present, makes things easier. But the lovableness is ultimately the God who is in them as He is in us, the God who does not override our personal identities but creates

and confirms them. So we don't find the other person lovable or attractive for God's sake (treating
God as a third party) but because God in the other
person has made him attractive in himself. And
because God is the deep centre of both us and the
other we find that we belong to each other in the
most intimate way. We find that we are more than
blood-brothers, most intimately interconnected in
the deep places of our being.

Listening may begin as a one-way operation, but
it can never be that for long. In the silence of our
listening we are communicating implicitly with the
other person in a language other than words, and
thus revealing to him what we are. And the time
will come when our self-revelation will become ver-
bally explicit. Our relationship will cease to be apparently one way, as if we were the Good
Samaritan and the other the wounded victim,
because we shall realize that in order to be healed
the other needs to see our own ugly wounds, to
encounter us in our sickness as well as in our health
just as we are beginning to encounter him in his
health as well as in his sickness. We shall discover
that both the sickness and the health are things we
have in common, so that both can become a bond
between us. And as in this way we share what we
are with each other we shall discover that it is in
each other that we live.

This can happen with regard to anybody to
whom we are prepared to listen and to go on listening. And it thus becomes apparent that each of us

belongs to all and all to each. It becomes apparent that we are not isolated self-enclosed units, but that the blood of all people throbs in our own veins as does ours in theirs. And the more a person realizes this fact of his co-inherence in others, the more he becomes his own true self. This, of course, is what St Paul was describing when he spoke of the Body of Christ, for Christ in God's eternal purpose is co-extensive with mankind (and indeed with the entire created universe)—"If one member suffers, all suffer together; if one member is honoured, all rejoice together." It is this oneness with each other that Eastern Orthodox thought expresses when it says that man has one single nature in many human persons. "Experience", says Thomas Merton, "is not mine. It is uninterrupted exchange. It is dance." And it is in being caught up in this dance of humanity, which is also the dance of the whole created universe, that a person discovers who he truly is.

As with a work of art, so also with other people. It is by the way of what we have called Intelligence that we know them, going out not only to meet them, but delving down deep into what they are, into their innermost reality, and finding there our own personal identity because it is God Himself who is their deepest centre and ground as He is also ours.

Something like a description of true identity found in other people and in all things was given by Rupert Brooke, though for what he calls "this

tumultuous body" we should read the false self with
its grasping, concupiscent, mind. We shall, he says,

"Spend in pure converse our eternal day;
Think each in each immediately wise;
Learn all we lacked before; hear, know, and
say,
What this tumultuous body now denies;
And feel who have laid our groping hands
away;
And see, no longer blinded by our eyes."

THE SNOB AND HIS POOR RELATIONS

One of the results of the discovery that we are not
isolated egos is that we are prepared to acknowledge
as our own and to befriend aspects of ourselves
which formerly we had tried to exclude from the
false fabricated self.

That self, as we saw, was under threat of loss.
And therefore in its anxiety it felt compelled to
disown a great deal of what in fact belonged to it as
a snob disowns his poor relations. The false
fabricated self tries to set itself up as a decent sort, a
good chap, one who can always be relied upon to
have the right attitude to things, a lover of goodness

and of God. And all those inner dispositions which go against this image of itself are locked away in a dark room. But people locked for any time in a dark room tend to bang at the door, and the banging makes the fabricated self even more anxious. The pity of it is that those locked up are not *au fond* destructive savages. With welcome understanding, and love, they would be capable of contributing valuably to what the person is, even if, by their nature, they can never be fully domesticated. Aggression, for instance, can be a powerfully creative force which enriches the world in all sorts of ways, even if it does sometimes spill over into fits of violent temper. In a charming and characteristically gentle letter to a close friend, Hans Andersen wrote:

"I feel a desire to be rude to somebody. I must have air! Would you do me the truly friendly favour of insulting me a little this evening, so that I may have cause to give vent to my rage, there's a kind soul! After all, I'm not asking something very difficult, am I?"

Jealousy is only a perverted form of the drive for the best; and to admit the drive involves the danger of its perversion to destructively self-centred ends. Learning (in T. S. Eliot's words) to care and not to care, learning to sit still, is sometimes the best and indeed only service we can render others, though behind it there always lurks the danger of sloth and indifference. Sexual feeling of the sort often socially unacceptable is the dynamic behind a great deal of what is best done (few school-teachers, for instance, can function fruitfully without it) though it always has in it the potentiality of turning destructively sour.

The fabricated self tries to exclude these dispositions and impulses from its empire for fear that they may turn into rebellious subjects. And collectivities, like churches, can do this as well as individuals. As Patrick White, the Australian novelist, wrote to some friends in 1970: "The churches defeat their own aims, I feel, through the banality of their approach, and by rejecting so much that is sordid and shocking which can still be related to religious experience. . . . I feel that the moral flaws in myself are more than anything my creative source."

The true self, however, is open to these disturbing influences, welcoming them as friends and allies. And since it has found its security in the loss of all securities (found it, that is, in God alone and His continuous creation of the self), the true self is not unduly worried by the disturbing and explosive. It is not worried by the occasional outburst of temper— "There is nothing worse than a bad temper," said Bishop Gore as he looked at William Temple's beaming face, "except a good one!" The true self is ready to receive, now and then, bouts of the most discomforting jealousy, and the possibility that it may be lazy or (in the conventional sense) lusting in its heart after somebody. It understands that the command of Jesus that we should be perfect as our heavenly Father is perfect can be obeyed only by means of our absolute trust in that same heavenly Father to make us perfect in His way, not in ours. And that in any case the word translated "perfect" here (*teleios*) means complete, full-grown, mature. The true self, because it trusts God to do what He has promised, has no need to be tortured by the mirages our hymns frequently hold up before us of our being "perfect and right and pure and good"— mirages which are perhaps the most blatant form of idolatry to which we are tempted. The true self, because it has realized its deepest centre in God, is not unduly perturbed to find that towards the periphery it is fragmented and messy. That is what it expects, for it is free from spiritual *folies de grandeur* and understands that it is still being created and that creation (as the scientists have shown us) is not a clean operation complete in seven days, but involves all sorts of false starts, dead ends and general mess over an immense period of time. So the true self does not bury its talents in the ground for fear. It accepts disarray as the price of creation. "Not the maximum of harmlessness," wrote von Hügel, "but the maximum of fruitfulness, together with what may be its unavoidable dangers, this is what we want."

Because the true self, unlike its fabricated caricature, is free from moralistic anxiety, it can find God in the superabundance of His Joy, knowing that His Joy is always a free gift and never a matter of desert.

WALKING ON THE WATER

Living our true selves as we continually flow from God's creative Joy is, more than anything, like walking on the water. We have no guarantees in the earthly sense of that word, no certificates of safety, certainly no explanations of how we do it. Our life is just a spontaneous walking with God. Once we begin to grow self-conscious and to look for our securities (earthly ones in fact, though we often think them spiritual because they are often ecclesiastical) we feel that we are sinking. The supreme Joy of our walking with God as if on water can be ours only if we are prepared to take a supreme risk. Yet in the end the risk is only to our fabricated self, so it doesn't really matter, however agonizingly it may feel it does.

"If you let it
  it supports itself
  you don't have to.

"Each something
  is a celebration
    of the nothing
    that supports it.

"When we
  remove the world from our
    shoulders·
  we notice it doesn't drop.
  Where is the responsibility?"

That may sound high-falutin and unpractical to the verge of dottiness. "Come down to earth," will be the cry. In fact we have never left earth, but we will take the point by referring to an English statesman· who walked with God. In Gwendolen Cecil's *Life of Robert Marquis of Salisbury*, her father, she tells of an occasion when, as Foreign Secretary, he received from guests and friends, at a moment of acute international crisis, expressions of sympathy on the terrible burden of responsibility he was carrying. When everybody had left he said to his family: "They would have been terribly shocked if I had told them the truth—which was that I did not understand what they were talking about." The family protested, and the story goes on:

> "He was about to start upon a walk and was standing at the moment at the open door, looking out on the threatening clouds of an autumn afternoon. 'I don't understand', he repeated, 'what people mean when they talk of the burden of responsibility. I should understand it if they spoke of the burden of decision—I feel it now, trying to make up my mind whether or no to take a great-coat with me. I feel it in exactly the same way, but no more, when I am writing a despatch upon

which peace or war may depend. Its degree
depends upon the materials for decision that are
available and not in the least upon the magnitude
of the results which may follow.' Then, after a
moment's pause and in a lower voice, he added
'With the results I have nothing to do.'"

THE FALSE SELF TAKES TO RELIGION AND FITS A HALO ON ITS HEAD

Because we are still half-in-halfers (though slowly
growing perhaps towards being three-quarterers)
we sometimes find ourselves using our experience of
our true selves to boost our false fabricated selves.
This can happen, for instance, in our experience of
God as we pray. Perhaps on occasion we have a
deep sense of God and of our flowing from Him.
Then the grasping concupiscent self pokes its head
up and claims the experience as a capital gain for its
empire. It tells itself that its religious empire is
growing nicely (to God be the glory, of course) and
that its possession of this empire is becoming more
secure. In His mercy God does not generally allow

this state of affairs to continue for long. If we are lucky He sends us dryness, absence of all feeling when we pray, so as to teach us that what flows from Him cannot thus be pocketed and capitalized. And thus He allows our true self room to grow by preventing the rebuilding of the fabricated self along what we may mistakenly consider to be spiritual lines.

What is true of spirituality is true also of morality. The demands of virtue are literally endless. If, as St Paul said, love is the fulfilling of the law, then the law's reach is without limit because love is. There is always something more we can think or say or do for others. This surely is the point of the parable of Jesus about the farmer who makes his labourer serve him supper at the end of the day's toil, and considers such service no ground for thanks. It is not that such behaviour on the part of employers is being praised or recommended, but that doing one's duty, however completely, still leaves one an unprofitable servant because the claims of goodness are without end. (Like our desires, they belong to the order of infinity.) Those who allow themselves to be persecuted by the parable into a neurotic perfectionism are thinking of it in terms of the false fabricated self which it is the purpose of the parable to break up by showing how impossible it is for a necessarily limited amount of moral capital to meet demands that are altogether without limit. Goodness, in other words, can spring only from God's continuous creative act within us. It is the harvest of the Spirit making inclination from within, and not a law from without, the basis of what we do. Perhaps the greatest miracle God ever performs is what Coleridge called the moralizing of the affections; making goodness attractive to us so that doing good things becomes the highest sort of pleasure in spite of all the effort and pain it may involve. This was the Joy set before him with which Jesus endured the cross.

Yet here again the false self will poke up its head and try to make capital for itself out of the good deeds we have done, trying to persuade us that we really are becoming rather virtuous people (again, of course, to God be the glory!). As J. B. Mozley, that wisest of counsellors, wrote in 1876:

"We may observe a tendency sometimes in persons of zeal and forwardness in religion to suppose that they can speak highly of their own spiritual gifts and graces, provided they do it with thankful acknowledgement that this goodness is the work of grace in them, and received from the Holy Spirit. But this is surely a very hazardous and inconsistent use to which they turn the dispensation of the Spirit, to use it as enabling persons to speak highly of their own state. . . . The great test of humility is our estimate of the fact of our condition. If this estimate is high, then to whatever origin we may attribute it, we do not practically fulfil the law laid down in the Gospel (in the parable of the Pharisee and the Publican).

Rather it is founding a species of self-righteousness on this very law."

It is not odd that those words, preached just over a hundred years ago, should speak so pertinently to our own day, since truth is always contemporary and the false fabricated self does not change much.

THE IMP

If the greatest miracle God ever does is the moralizing of the affections, then one of the greatest gifts He can give us is what could be called the Imp.

The Imp is not the Fiend. He is not malicious or cynical. But he loves to poke fun at the pretensions of the false self and make us laugh about them. He is a sort of internalized court jester who jokes us out of being the heavy-minded bores we have it in us to be. He goes with us everywhere, dancing about in the most unseemly fashion, making rude faces at us, mimicking our inward gestures in absurd caricature and saying the most outrageous things. Pompous people may try to tame him by calling him the angel of the ludicrous, but he answers by asking us whether we always use seven syllables when one will do. "I suppose", he says, "that you always say terminological inexactitude when you mean a lie. I'm not an angel of anything. I'm an Imp."

Here we can notice that among God's many great gifts to Pope John the Imp was by no means the least important. The Imp within Pope John often bewildered and scandalized the staid bureaucrats of the Vatican and other pious personages in Rome. His antics are too many and well known to be recorded here, though perhaps one of his performances may be described as typical of the rest: "One day Pope John visited the Hospital of the Holy Spirit in Rome which is administered by a religious sisterhood. The mother superior, stirred by the papal visitation, went up to him in order to introduce herself: 'Most Holy Father, I am the Superior of the Holy Spirit,' she said. 'Well, I must say you're lucky,' replied the Pope. 'I'm only the Vicar of Jesus Christ.' "

The Imp within us can be particularly active when we are at our prayers. Just when we are beginning to congratulate ourselves on our spiritual wealth he prostrates himself full-length on the floor, his hands stretched out in the most ridiculous way, the very picture of melodramatic devotion in a corny play. And as if that didn't make us laugh enough, he gets up from the floor and imitates the irritation we show when somebody calls just as our favourite television serial is about to start. Finding us feeling that we love all mankind, the Imp in perfect mimicry repeats our own words in our own voice: "Damn the man. I wish he'd go and live in Timbuctoo."

Or if we feel we've done something rather generous and thus increased our moral capital, the Imp puts on the face and posture of a small child who has been told that Father Christmas will only visit him if he's been good. And in a childish treble the Imp will repeat several times: "I'm not a naughty boy. I'm a good boy."

Or if we are feeling a little depressed and dramatize ourselves as somebody caught up in the giant agony of the world, the Imp puts on his counter-act of a ham tragedian reciting Sydney Carton's farewell: "Ah, do not grieve for me, but think of me as one who died young whose life might have been. But my life has been but an empty dream, a dream that ends in nothing and leaves the poor sleeper where he first lay down."

The Imp in his performances often uses snatches of popular songs, ancient and modern. One of his favourites when we're feeling especially holy is "I'm dancing with tears in my eyes". Or when we catch ourselves thinking that we have attained a certain degree of child-like simplicity, he sings: "What's going to happen to the children when there aren't any more grown-ups?" Or if some cowardly fear makes us run for shelter to the respectability we miscall prudence or virtue, the Imp begins singing:

"Don't tell my mother I'm living in sin / Don't let the old folks know / Don't tell my twin that I breakfast on gin / She'd never survive the blow."

"After the ball is over" is one of the Imp's favourites

when we go from our prayers to the daily irritants of life, while if we're feeling orthodox in a particularly militant way, he sings:

"We don't want to fight,
But by Jingo if we do
We've got the Faith, we've got the Mass,
We've got the Maleness too."

It is a curious thing—the effect the Imp has on us. We love him because he makes us laugh, but in doing that he is often a tear-jerker as well. That is because while ridiculing us as denizens of the far country of our false selves, he also reminds us that our Father's home, where we can know the joy of being what we truly are, is always open to us.

MAN THE CREATOR

If Joy is ultimately God, who is its source, then our experience of Joy will not be a passive intake of all good for the self, but an active concern for a good to be realized.

We say of God that in His creation He realizes a good. And as He is the deepest centre and ground of our true selves, we shall, in Him, set out in our turn to create some good or value. There can be no Joy where there is no creativity because the absence of creativity is a denial of Joy at its source, that is, a denial of God the Creator.

That means that we must all be poets if we are to be what God intends us to be—not, of course, poets as we now understand the word (very few of us can be that), but in its original sense of makers.

One of the paradoxes of life is that all the best gifts, although freely given, have to be worked for. A man, for instance, may be born a genius, but he has to work devastatingly hard in order to actualize what is in him. A lazy genius is a contradiction in terms. Or the deep love of two people for each other is a gift absolutely, but a lot of work has to go into it if it is to prosper and mature. And although, from one point of view, all we can do is continually to receive from our Creator what we are, from another viewpoint this very receiving is an activity which requires the utmost discipline and dedication. We have, in St Paul's words, to work out our own salvation even if it is God who is at work in us. As Thomas Traherne reminds us:

"A quiet Mind is worse than Poverty
   Unless it from Enjoyment spring.
   That's Blessedness alone that makes a King!
   Wherein the Joyes and Treasures are so great,
   They all the powers of the Soul employ,
   And fill it with a Work Compleat,
   While it doth all enjoy.
   Life! Life is all: in its most full extent
   Stretcht out to all things, and with all Content!"

It is in this sense that we all need to be poets or makers. And if, in this paradoxical way, we all have to be the makers of ourselves, we cannot accomplish that work without creating something of public value, that is, of value for others, because (as we have seen) it is only by going out to the other that we find ourselves—the mystery which in the Godhead is pointed to by the doctrine of the Trinity.

If therefore a man is to find the Joy which is his true self he will need to actualize what he is, we could say incarnate what he is, in some particular thing or doubtless in a great number of particular things. The majority of people are not artists in the technical sense that they paint, compose or write (except as side-lines or hobbies), but they are artists, poets, or makers in the wider sense that they embody their potentialities in various concrete forms as lovers, spouses, parents, friends and workers, whatever their job may be. In all these ways they are active for a good or value to be realized. And it is thus that God's unlimited creativity finds its expression in this or that particular and limited form.

The central place of creativity in man's true being is witnessed to in such phrases as "it is better to travel hopefully than to arrive" or "a man's reach should exceed his grasp" or "what's a heaven for?" Man, to be truly himself, needs always more space than that which he is at present occupying because he is by nature a creator and his universe needs always to be able to expand. Love, for instance, is always looking for new idioms of expression as circumstances change: a son aged twenty is not to be loved in the same way as a son aged five. The tendency shown by people who are keen on their job to reform and improve the way things are done witnesses to the same creative urge. There is no Joy in stagnation because it is a denial of what God is, and hence of what we truly are.

One of the less obvious, but none the less fundamental, aspects of the false fabricated self is that it tends to put together a pattern of how things are, or of what they should aim to be, and then cling to it as a limpet to a rock. The false self is not open to the present which is becoming the future. In Gabriel Marcel's phrase, it is "tarnished by catalogued experience" because it does not apprehend the creative power in which it lives and has its being, the power of bringing forth what is new. It thinks of life as perpetual repetition and consequently imagines that old solutions will solve new problems because the problems are not really new at all. It is an attitude which could be called the pathology of conservatism. Or, instead of reverting to old solutions, the false self may in despair conclude that there will never be any solutions because those in the past have always failed to work.

There is a fundamental distinction between, on the one hand, a mechanic and, on the other, an inventor. The mechanic tends the machine according to the book of instructions. If the design of the machine is faulty and the book of instructions is thus of no use, the mechanic is at the end of his resources. But the inventor insists that there must be a way in which the machine can be designed so that it works properly and that he is going to find it. He appeals to the creative power within him and thereby discovers how a properly functioning machine can be made.

The true self is an inventor, not a mechanic. And it is in the use of its inventive creative powers that it finds Joy. It refuses to be held down under the crust of habit. It destroys habit by hope. It has a mind open to surprises.

To create is not (as we noticed earlier) an easy, clean and clear-cut process. It is generally a prolonged and messy business. The moment of inspiration, wrote J. N. Figgis, "is the end, not the beginning—it is the flash of insight that comes at the end of long, almost hopeless toil, the brilliant vision which is the reward of torments both of body and spirit". Whatever the dimension in which we are working, we cannot share the Joy of God's creativity without also sharing in its cost and pain, revealed, so Christians believe, in Christ crucified. So it is hope above all things that we need as we travel through the night of doubt and sorrow to whatever may be the particular articulation of the Promised Land we are concerned about. Hope is a generous friend because, when we entertain her, she enables us to find the unhoped-for—something better and more gloriously satisfying than anything we had imagined at the start.

INFINITY REVEALED
WITHIN BOUNDS

The effort and pain of creativity lies very largely in its needing to capture the universal in a particular form. Karl Jaspers has defined poetry as "infinity grown self-contained". He was thinking of poetry in the usual technical sense, but what he says applies to all the making we have to do.

It is beauty or reality which the artist (in the technical sense) has to capture and encapsulate. But the same thing has to be done for universal qualities like goodness, righteousness, love, peace, patience, and so on. These qualities are utterly void and impotent if they are only floating in the air. They have to be brought down to earth and embodied if they are to be effective. And it is the effort to embody them which constitutes the toil and pain of creativity. How can the truest love, for instance, embody itself in a particular situation which is both tricky and subtle? The answer is by no means obvious and it will require much sweat, much Deliberation, to discover.

And not only Deliberation, but the ability to endure the possibility that the answer we arrive at may well be a mistake. Did not part of the agony of Jesus in Gethsemane consist in his awareness of the haunting possibility that there may have been some fundamental mistake in the embodiment he had tried to give to the kingdom of God? Tolerance of that possibility is the price which must always be paid for creativity.

Yet if in the end we discover that there was no mistake, we learn something infinitely glorious about the potentialities of our limited world. We learn that what is limited is not imprisoned within its limits, that imperfection is not the negation of perfection, that infinity can be revealed within bounds. Who when contemplating some magnificent view or some masterpiece of painting, ever asks for more beauty? *There can be no more beauty* because beauty itself has been captured and revealed within the limits of the view or painting concerned. Who, when he reads of Sonia's utterly faithful love for Raskolnikov, can ask for more love? For infinite love is embodied within the limits of Sonia's person. Is it not along these lines that the mystery of the Incarnation should be approached? To the degree in which men share in God's creativity, to that degree the eternal is manifested within the limits of time, the abiding within the limits of the evanescent, the supernatural within the limits of the natural. That is a common daily experience. The gist of it has been well put by Miss E. M. Almedingen in her biography of Grand-Duchess Serge of Russia: "She never argued about her faith, but she possessed the very rare gift of coming to the heart of the matter where all things created became music to her within the concept of the Incarnation." And it is precisely with this music of Joy that we are concerned throughout this book.

Good and Bad Art

One other point needs noticing about God's creativity at work through us. It will certainly require a great deal of what we have called Deliberation. A poet or maker is a craftsman and the exercise of every craft involves a great deal of working things out. But the reality we embody can be apprehended only by what we have called Intelligence, the coming to the heart of the matter, the entering into what we apprehend so that it becomes part of our own identity. It is sometimes called vision, and we can in this connection remember what G. K. Chesterton said about the Victorian painter G. F. Watts—that his right hand taught him terrible things.

Words, however, are a nuisance because they often have different meanings. What we have called Deliberation is often referred to as the discursive intellect. And it is in that sense that Iris Murdoch uses the phrase in a warning we should do well to ponder: "Good art", she says, "accepts and celebrates the defeat of the discursive intellect by the world. Bad art falsifies the world so as to pretend that there is no such defeat."

By what we have called Intelligence we apprehend transcendent value—beauty, for instance, or love. By some sort of miracle people are able to capture and embody infinite value in a limited and finite medium—a painting or a loving family. And the miracle is assisted by our ability to put two and two together and work things out—i.e., by our powers of Deliberation. But when the miracle has been accomplished, the result is not at all what our calculations have led us to expect. It does not appear as we have worked it out. To see what is meant you have only to compare a photograph of something with the same thing painted by Van Gogh or Monet. The painting defiantly and triumphantly declares that the object concerned is not what our powers of Deliberation (our discursive intellect) took it to be. Hence the uproar and vilification with which a new idiom in painting is invariably assailed. The protest goes up that things are not like that. If the painter is faithful to his vision he may in the end persuade people that things *are* like that, however much his paintings contradict our ordinary mental concepts of those things. If, on the other hand, the painter is chicken-hearted, he will pretend in his paintings that things do correspond adequately with our ordinary mental concepts of them, and produce chocolate-box art.

But suppose the transcendent value to be embodied is love in, as we have suggested, a loving family. We shall have worked out all sorts of things that should or shouldn't happen in a loving family. But the love so embodied may well play absolute havoc with our most reasonable notions and calculations. The loving family may be completely different from what we expected it to be as reality triumphantly takes over from convention. And then the cry will go up: "Why can't we be like other families?"—a cry which is the parallel to the demand for chocolate-box art.

The Closed Door is the Passageway

Goodness embodied in act or speech is invariably disturbing and often shocking. It has about it an intransigent quality, which refuses to compromise and can therefore often be mistaken for its opposite, as happened, for instance, in the condemnation on moral grounds of Socrates and Jesus. The transcendent values (goodness and truth) embodied within the limits of a human person were too uncomfortable and disruptive to be tolerated.

Don Cupitt has spoken of "Jesus' ironical perception of *disjunction* between the things of God and the things of men", and sees in this perception of disjunction the basis of "Christianity's proper subtlety". But Cupitt has underrated the subtlety. Jesus taught that the things of God are indeed embodied in the things of men; that human fatherhood, for instance, can show us something of divine fatherhood. But when the things of God are thus embodied in the things of men, although the things of men still remain human, the humanness thus displayed begins to look a bit odd—as odd in fact as did the brush-strokes of Van Gogh and Monet when they first appeared on canvas. What, therefore, we have is both continuity *and* disjunction, and it is this combination which is the real subtlety of Christianity.

The point may seem merely academic, but in reality it is crucial to any understanding of God as Joy. The world, it has been said, is the closed door. It is a barrier and at the same time it is the passageway. The world is the closed door and barrier before we have discovered God's Joy within us, since then there is nothing in us to go out to His Joy in the world, which seems in consequence no more than an inveterate lump of existence. But when God's Joy has awoken within us the world becomes the passageway to His Joy everywhere. And the passageway may then lead us into what our rational calculations may describe as any sort of hell and high water. For to dance for the Joy of God is often to find ourselves at variance with our reasonable expectations (not to mention our natural inclinations), being carried by the dance, like St Peter, whither we would not.

SUFFERING AND JOY

If, when we dance for Joy (God's Joy), we may well be carried whither we would not, then His Joy in us may well involve suffering. An attempt must therefore be made to explore the relation between the two.

That relation is part of what is called the problem of evil. We shall not, however, be concerned with that problem as such—trying to justify the ways of God to man. Our concern will be narrower. We shall attempt to observe how in human experience Joy can be involved in suffering and suffering in Joy. For the two are by no means mutually exclusive as superficial estimates of the human condition tend to suppose.

For Christians the archetypal pattern of the relationship between Joy and suffering must always remain Christ's passion, death and resurrection. But for most Christians these unfathomable mysteries have become little more than notions about which they appear to speak with an ease that borders on an almost pert loquacity. It is a state of affairs well described by Coleridge: "Truths of all others the most awful and mysterious and at the same time of universal interest, are considered as so true as to lose all the powers of truth, and lie bed-ridden in the dormitory of the soul." Because this is unfortunately the case, we shall as far as possible avoid speaking of Christ's passion, death and resurrection and try to discover how that one great mystery works itself out in terms of the experience of ordinary people.

That there is often an ambiguity in people's experience of suffering is well attested. Florence

Farmborough, for instance, has published the diaries she wrote as a nursing sister at the Russian Front in the First World War. She subsequently travelled a great deal around the world, but in the preface to her book she writes: "When I am asked: 'Which land did you love most?', unhesitatingly I answer: 'Russia, because she taught me the meaning of the word "suffering"'." Similarly Van Gogh wrote: "It always strikes me, and it is very peculiar, that whenever we see the image of indescribable and unutterable desolation—of loneliness, poverty, and misery, the end and extreme of all things—the thought of God comes into one's mind."

From here we are led inevitably to the attraction of tragedy as a dramatic form, a topic about which countless volumes have been written. It will suffice to mention two representative statements: "Our sympathy in tragic fiction", wrote Shelley, "depends on this principle: tragedy gives delight by affording a shadow of the pleasure which exists in pain." "A poet", wrote W. B. Yeats, "creates tragedy from his own soul which is alike in all men. It has not joy, as we understand that word, but ecstasy, which is from the contemplation of things vaster than the individual and imperfectly seen, perhaps by all those who still live."

There is a knife-edge here from which one can easily fall into banality—a banality deliciously satirized by W. S. Gilbert when his forlorn maidens, on eventually returning to their first true loves, are made to sing:

"The pain that is all but a pleasure will
  change
For the pleasure that's all but pain."

But the ambiguity often found in the experience of
suffering none the less remains.
  How are we to account for it?
  We cannot account for it fully and least of all in a
way that can be codified for ready understanding.
And in this area more than in all others we must
avoid the easy speeches which comfort cruel men.
Suffering is too terrible to be trifled with. But certain tentative approaches can none the less be made.
  There is, first of all, the psycho-pathology known
as masochism, in which intense pleasure is derived
from intense pain, so that the pain is actively sought
for the pleasure it brings. This can be dismissed at
once. The suffering with which we are concerned is
not sought after. It comes when our prayer "Let this
cup pass from me" is answered in a manner contrary to our desire. Of course religious people (like
everybody else) can be masochists and they should
be aware of the possibility of masochism lurking
unknown in this or that pocket of what they are.
There is something in Norman Douglas's jibe at the
religious sect he planted in his island of Nepenthe.
They were prepared, he said, to carry out to the
letter the difficult injunctions of their faith "since it
gave them what all religious people require—
something to torment themselves with". But that is
an acknowledged caricature. There is no masochism

in sufferings which are not only uninvited but which
we cannot stop however completely we return to
psychic health.

A more promising approach is the necessarily
ambiguous nature of all sensibility. When, after
twenty years' absence, Henry James returned to
New York and found his old home pulled down and
replaced, it was his eye for architecture which led
him to complain of the replacement that it was "a
high square impersonal building, proclaiming its
lack of interest with a crudity all its own". In the
same way a person with a sensitive ear for music
will be hurt by the noise of a road drill outside
much more than a person whose aural sensitivity
allows him to use music as no more than a background noise for chatter. Or a person who gets deep
pleasure from an atmosphere he feels and knows is
authentic will be correspondingly harassed by its
opposite, as, for instance, John Betjeman:

> "It's not their fault they do not know
> The birdsong from the radio,
> It's not their fault they often go
> To Maidenhead

> "And talk of sports and makes of cars
> In various bogus Tudor bars
> And daren't look up and see the stars
> But belch instead."

In all these cases sensibility is ambiguous, the
capacity for pain being the inevitable concomitant

of the capacity for delight. Suffering is here shown as the twin-sister of joy.

It is also true that the deeper a man's sensibility goes the more isolated he will become because fewer and fewer people will be able to share his vision. When (as we have seen) von Hügel wrote: "the deeper you go the more alone you will find yourself", he was speaking as a man whose spiritual sensibilities had gone so deep that few if any could understand the universe he inhabited.

When, however, von Hügel went on to say that religion had never made him comfy, that he had been in the desert ten years, that all deepened life was deepened suffering, deepened dreariness, deepened Joy, he was speaking of something different from his inability to share his deepest experiences with others. And much can be learnt from a consideration of his words.

First we can notice that the deeper we go down within ourselves the more do we discover those elements of us which (as we saw) the false self tends to disown as a snob disowns his poor relations. And what we are compelled to do is not only to recognize and acknowledge these apparently nasty things but to assimilate them so that they can provide energy for our true selves. This process of acknowledgement and assimilation is hardly likely to make a man comfy. It will disturb and pain him. Yet it is to this task that religion, in von Hügel's sense, calls us. But there is more than that to going deeper.

One of the ways in which small children learn to

relate to their world is by means of toys—teddy-
bears and so on. God in His love gives us what may
be described as spiritual toys in order that we may
learn to relate to Him—chiefly pictures of Himself
as this or that which at first are highly evocative. But
God is greater and other than our pictures of Him
as a real human person is greater and other than a
teddy-bear. So in order to further our growth towards spiritual maturity, God slowly takes away from
us one by one the evocative pictures He had in the
first instance given to us. And in consequence we
are left feeling desolate like a small child robbed of
its teddy-bear. And as the evocative power of each
picture dies on us we feel to that extent dreary and
in the desert. Our devotional feelings pack up on us
and we apparently find no pleasure at all in our
communion with God. But that is a necessary
prelude (how long it lasts is God's business, not
ours; it may last until the day of our death) to our
discovering the Joy which is God Himself so that it
may replace the pleasure we once obtained from the
pictures of Him. The word "prelude" here can be
misleading. For the Joy which is God Himself may
be apprehended—however dimly in the background—at the same time as we feel sharply in the
foreground the absence of our former pleasure. It is
as if, having immensely enjoyed the operettas of
Johann Strauss and Franz Lehar, we were bundled
into Bayreuth for Wagner's Ring cycle. We miss the
catchy tunes, the easy rhythms, the sentimental
songs, and are exposed instead to what at first seems

no more than mere deadening noise. Yet gradually we begin on occasions to be aware of the possibility of a profound exultation, a superlative experience, totally lacking in our former favourite song: "You are my heart's delight", or whatever. Yet what we may have for the time being is the awareness only of a possibility of exultation, a possibility we are not yet capable of assimilating properly, let alone of sorting out; and we may find ourselves in amused agreement with Mark Twain in thinking that Wagner's music is better than it sounds. So in our first sessions at Bayreuth deprivation and superabundance, suffering and joy, will be mixed. And the suffering will be the very context of the joy. Our sadly missing Johann Strauss and Franz Lehar will be the occasion of our envisaging the possibility of gaining much greater riches from Wagner.

That is the kind of condition the spiritual writers call faith. They understand that the awareness of the possibility of God's Joy is often the form in which we experience the Joy itself. Hence de Caussade says:

"Faith is never unhappy even when the senses are most desolate. This lively faith is always in God, always in His action above contrary appearances by which the senses are darkened. The senses, in terror, suddenly cry to the soul 'Unhappy one! You have no resources. You are lost,' and instantly faith with a stronger voice answers: 'Keep firm, go on, fear nothing.'"

That is how von Hügel could say ". . . suffering and joy. The final note of religion is joy."

The exposure here, however, is not only to God but also to His world, where, at the deepest levels, agony and ecstasy are so closely intertwined. The more we discern God's Joy everywhere the greater will be our sensitivity to the cost and pain by which the Joy has been brought about. We remember the woman in travail who has sorrow because her hour is come. The more we enter into the Joy of God's creation the more shall we experience the sorrow of its birth pangs. Few people, for instance, were so aware of God's glory in His world as Gerard Manley Hopkins: "The world is charged with the grandeur of God. It will flame out." "Glory be to God for dappled things," and so on. But the cost of it was all but intolerable because it involved his experiencing a darkness almost as great as the light:

> "O the mind, mind has mountains; cliffs of fall
> Frightful, sheer, no-man-fathomed. Hold them cheap
> May who ne'er hung there."

We have already mentioned St Francis of Assisi and his recognition of God's Joy everywhere. It was no coincidence that he bore the stigmata. Perfect Joy and perfect affliction have a mysterious unity. That is why to know the Joy is to be vulnerable to the affliction, while in the affliction we can be aware of at least the possibility of Joy.

Yet the dreadful heart of the matter has not yet been plumbed. For suffering is at its most terrible when it delivers not even the faintest hint of the possibility of Joy. In all sorts of forms, in terms of mind, body or estate, suffering can descend upon a person and completely overwhelm him so that he becomes one wide wound—all of him. When we encounter such suffering in somebody, at one level of our being it is natural for us to flee it—at least by explaining it away as Job's friends tried to do. Yet on a deeper level we recognize something of infinite significance and of infinite worth, something sacred, in the utter desolation such suffering brings. Lionel Trilling suggested that it was in his estimation of this dimension of suffering that Sigmund Freud reached closest to an attitude which could be called religious:

"Nothing could be further from my intention than to suggest that Freud's attitude to human experience is religious. I have it in mind only to point to the analogy which may be drawn from Freud's response to life and an attitude which, although it is neither exclusive to nor definitive of religion, is yet, as it were, contained by religion and sustained by it. This is what we might call the tragic element in Judaism and Christianity, having reference to the actual literary genre of tragedy and its inexplicable power to activate, by the representation of suffering, a faith quite unrelated to hope, a piety which takes virtually the form of pride—however harsh and seemingly gratuitous a fate may be, the authenticity of its implicit significance is not to be denied, confirmed as it is by the recognition of *some* imperative which has brought it into being and prescribed its acceptance, and in doing so has affirmed the authenticity of him to whom the fate is assigned. It is this authenticating imperative, irrational and beyond the reach of reason, that Freud wishes to preserve."

Suffering as Trilling here speaks of it reminds us of what Iris Murdoch said about art: "Good art accepts and celebrates the defeat of the discursive intellect by the world. Bad art falsifies the world so as to pretend that there is no such defeat."

In the Bible this theme is worked out most fully in the Book of Job. Job's friends try to find reasons for his sufferings, to domesticate them within the four walls of some rational world view of transgression and retribution. They thus represent bad art. Job himself steadfastly refuses this way out. There is no explanation why his sufferings have befallen him. They cannot be contained within any rationally satisfying system of ideas. In the end, when the Lord appears to him in a whirlwind, Job accepts his fate without trying any more to understand why it has befallen him. And in this acceptance what is revealed to us is his authenticity. Job stands out as a real person while his friends are seen as no more than cardboard figures. What Job comes to see, writes D. Z. Phillips, "is that he does not know. . . . He is saying that things are unknowable. . . . To acknowledge that he did not know was for Job the solution, or rather, the dissolution, of his questions; to see all things in the hand of God."

When, therefore, we say that Job is finally revealed to us in his authenticity as the man who acknowledges that things are unknowable, what we may be suggesting is that Job is revealed to us as someone whom nothing can separate from the love of God. For the love of God cannot be known in terms of bad chocolate-box art. The characteristic of the love of God is that it surpasses knowledge as good art does. Hence to accept unknowability, as Job did, may be a form of accepting God's love, and thus of apprehending His Joy, even when it comes to us savagely out of the whirlwind in the midst of our intensest sufferings—sufferings whose *raison d'être* we cannot begin to understand.

"Only the very greatest art", says Iris Murdoch, "invigorates without consoling." God's love can be compared to the very greatest art. It is not its *métier* to console, but to give life. One of the ways in which we desecrate the supreme mystery of Christ's death and resurrection is to turn it into bad chocolate-box art whose main, if not indeed only, function is to console. Christ's resurrection thus becomes something very like the conventional happy ending to a story where the characters live happily ever after within what looks suspiciously like the dimensions of this present historical world-order. The result is that within this order Joy and suffering come to be regarded as opposites instead of the correlatives they truly are, that is, different sides of the same coin.

The New Testament tells us always to give thanks for everything. Kierkegaard said that this possibility of giving thanks is part of the eternity which God has put in men's hearts. He meant that we do not give thanks as a result of the way things go, for the way things go is contingent. It is uncertain. Things may go any way. "But the Christian thanks God whatever happens, in the sense that nothing can render loving God pointless." Our capacity thus always to thank God is the Joy which He has given us and which nothing can take away.

Simone Weil is as aware as Iris Murdoch of the seduction of bad art. She writes:

"The question of Beaumarchais: 'Why these things rather than others?' never has any answer because the world is devoid of finality. The absence of finality is the reign of necessity. Things have causes and not ends. Those who think to discern special designs of Providence are like professors who give themselves up to what they call the explanation of the text, at the expense of a beautiful poem."

The poem with which we are here concerned is the natural order, as, labouring like a machine, it lies under the law of cause and effect. While doing this it also sleeps like a picture. So the beauty that the natural order reveals to us is the result of its lying under the law of cause and effect. Trees, for instance, grow according to this law and trees are beautiful. But the law of cause and effect can also catch us up in suffering, in its operation on our minds or psyches no less than upon our bodies. As citizens of the created order we are not immune from its law of cause and effect. But we are not thereby separated from its beauty. On the contrary, suffering reveals that we are bone of its bone and flesh of its flesh because it is the same law (of cause and effect) which is responsible both for the beauty and for the suffering.

That is the true mystery of Christ's passion:

"Faithful Cross! above all other,
   One and only noble tree!
None in foliage, none in blossom,
   None in fruit thy peer may be;
Sweetest wood and sweetest iron!
   Sweetest weight is hung on thee."

ACTION

"Few lips would be moved to song if they could find a sufficiency of kissing," says Rudyard Kipling's Eustace Cleever, a novelist of fame, as he meets officers just back from Burma. He means that they have done something, while he has only written.

One can understand Cleever's feelings in the atmosphere of returning heroes, but the antithesis he describes is false. Song and kissing spring from each other. A man's personal capacity to create can find satisfying expression in public action, while the public action can feed his personal capacity to create. Cleever's is a very old mistake against which, in various forms, a number of Christian mystics have protested. We can take the fourteenth-century Heinrich Suso as representative: "He who finds the inward in the outward goes deeper than he who only finds the inward in the inward." Action is not the antithesis of contemplation. It is contemplation's fruit and fuel, even if action can be the fuel only if it has first been the fruit. Otherwise it becomes activism—action for its own sake.

We have seen how Joy is God himself in us as we recognize and go out to meet His Joy around us. That happens when a person realizes his solidarity with the natural world, with the products of human creativity, and, most of all, with other people—in the time of their wealth but especially in the time of their tribulation. It is this co-inherence of all in each and each in all which the Joy of God reveals, and, by revealing, creates.

If, however, this has been the gist of our song, what about the kissing?

Kissing nowadays has become more or less compulsory, and we should be thankful that it is. Whatever is propounded we want to know its practical consequences for the public sector of our lives, that is, for the society in which we live. How should our insights find expression in public action? That is the question we can no longer evade now that we have all been to school with Karl Marx. It is not enough to interpret the world. Our business is to change it. Presumably this has been an implication of Christianity since Jesus, in St John's gospel, spoke of *doing* the truth. But Christians have often tended to confine doing the truth to the sphere of private personal ethics to the neglect of its meaning for public affairs. Marx's criticisms of Christianity, in so far as they are valid, have now made that impossible.

Invisible Action

The deepest and most important change will come about to the degree in which individual men and women appropriate God's Joy within and around them. For since we are all most deeply interconnected, an individual's appropriation of God's Joy will have repercussions that will extend to all mankind. To deny that fact is to deny the possibility of prayer, and to count things visible as the only reality. Christians who quite rightly follow Marx in his demand for practical results in the management of public affairs are sometimes, in their enthusiasm, led beyond this to the assumption that the only action is observable public action. But that is a denial of the invisible God; or at least it is the absurdity of supposing that He can work only within the confines of the social machinery with which we provide Him. It is one thing to be willing to learn from Marx; it is another to make God Himself into a Marxist. In the 1970s God still moves in a mysterious way His wonders to perform just as much as He did at Olney in the 1770s. For God Himself does not change even if our spiritual sensibilities do.

An incurable invalid who has accepted the pain of his constriction as his share in Christ's cross may do more to establish justice in the world than a host of bustling reformers. By accepting his pain generously and dedicating it freely to God as a continuous prayer for others, the sufferer can be the agent through whom God's creative and transforming love is shed abroad in the world. For God accepts and uses his dedication (however little he may often feel dedicated) to empower others to do great things. The people who in public life help to establish righteousness on the earth are debtors to those who support them by the hidden dedication of their lives. What is here being described is what St Paul called the mystery of Christ's Body, which with Him continually dies and, with Him, is also continually raised from the dead. That is why St Paul understood that "the weapons of our warfare are not worldly but have divine power to destroy strongholds". By voluntarily accepting the cruel necessity of his affliction as his share in Christ's passion, the sufferer brings to bear upon the world the power of Christ's resurrection which is His power of making all things new. We need to be reminded of this if we are not, in Rupert Brooke's phrase, to be blinded by our eyes. God still works to change His world for the better by means of the things which are not seen. By underlining the importance of public action to improve the economic structure of society so that a greater degree of justice might prevail, Marx has expanded our spiritual sensibilities, or at least has reminded Christians of what many of them had forgotten. We can gratefully allow him to do that without at the same time allowing him fatally to contract our spiritual sensibilities in another direction.

Joy and the Structures of Society

When we consider the implications for society of any great truth, all we can do is indicate the general direction in which that truth seems to point. We cannot go into details. For the details require expertise of various kinds and are in any case a matter of contingency in the sense that they will depend very largely upon a society's political, economic and cultural development (which in any society will not itself be homogeneous), with the result that any one specific proposal made will immediately be countered by dozens of others, as readers of *The Times* correspondence columns can see every day.

When, therefore, we investigate the implications for society of the Joy of God we shall not be drawing

up a detailed programme of action like the mani-
festo of a political party before an election. Our
concern will be with fundamental principles, not
with the specific way in which they should be
articulated; though we may sometimes be foolhardy
enough to make some particular concrete proposal,
partly by way of example and partly to be
provocative in the positive sense of provoking
thought. But our basic concern will remain the
great end of trying to see how society can be so
organized that men and women may be given the
maximum opportunity to discover God's Joy and
abide in it.

One caveat, however, needs to be entered at
once. The end never justifies the means. The means
must justify themselves. In other words, if we wish
to bring about a state of affairs in society whereby
men may be free to find God's Joy by finding their
true selves (as we have described it above) we cannot do this by means which even temporarily rob
them of their fundamental freedom or in any way
deny their humanity. For that is the lie on which all
inhuman tyranny is based—men must be forced
and tortured into a conformity that (it is claimed)
will result in some future common good. Even in
what is called a liberal democracy that sort of danger is not entirely absent. The role of the state in
protecting its citizens from whatever interferes with
or endangers their capacity to grow freely into the
inheritance of their humanity can be perverted into
governments and politicians deciding what is good

for people and then, by this way or that, forcing them into the chosen mould. True, that is a trick which the state has learnt from the practice of the Church in past ages. But it cannot be the means whereby a society enables its members to discover God's Joy for themselves.

In what general direction, then, must we move for that end to be attained?

Work

A man, we said, can discover God's Joy in the self-giving which his work entails—or should entail. For we noticed previously that one of the basic problems in an industrial society is the simple fact that the work of a man on an assembly line does not provide him with anything like adequate opportunity for self-giving and that this inevitably causes discontent and unrest. Experienced industrial chaplains say that in a well-run factory there can be a certain sense of community and that this is humanizing, but that it generally doesn't go very far. Marx thought that he had the answer to the problem in the collective ownership of the industrial plant. If society itself owned the factory, the worker in it would feel as if he were digging his own back-garden. This has proved a psychological fallacy if collective owner-ship means state ownership. For the industrial plant is still run by a set of directing bureaucrats; only the workers' paymaster has changed. The deadening impersonality remains. Ideally, perhaps, collective ownership would mean that everybody working in the factory would have a say in how it is run. But the realities of life are seldom ideal. Most workers are hesitant to share the burden of management for the very sensible reason that they realize that management is a highly skilled business for which they are not equipped.

Yet it must remain spiritually and morally wrong to cut men off from God's Joy in their work. It is no answer to quote Genesis: "In the sweat of thy brow shalt thou eat bread." For if this is the necessary curse under which humankind must labour, what have the middle and professional classes done to deserve liberation from it? True, they sometimes have tedious jobs or at least jobs that involve a considerable amount of tedious labour. But, on the whole, their jobs engage their interest even if the work is hard and has its elements of boredom. A man on an assembly line cannot give himself to his work as, for instance, an accountant can in his office or a traveller recommending the products of his firm. We seem in this matter to be the slaves of the past, assuming that things must be organized as, since modern industry started, they always have been.

Perhaps what at first sight looks like a threatening blanket of despair may turn out to be a ray of hope. As industry becomes more technological and automation requires only one person to do what previously was done by ten or twenty people, unemployment will grow to gigantic proportions. This terrible threat may goad us into a fundamental reappraisal of how work in industry should be organized, calling for the utmost effort of mind and imagination on the part of statesmen, economists, sociologists, industrial managers and trades union heads. The time may come when the only solution to the scourge of unemployment will be a two-day week for the workers in many industries. This would allow them to spend the other three days in pursuit of a craft or skill which engaged them fully. The problems of working out such a system would admittedly be immense, requiring radical changes in economic practice—in the matter, for instance, of wages and job distribution, not to mention the enormously difficult political problem of persuading the public to accept the changes suggested. But such things cannot be beyond the power of determined human contrivance. Necessity has ever been the mother of invention and where there is a will there is generally a way, even if it takes a long time to discover and the approach to it is beset with both controversy and conflict. After all, the economic and industrial system was made for man, not man for the system. The horror of rising unemployment may force us to see that we can change the system fundamentally for the better rather than having to accept it as inevitable.

A two-day week in a vast industrial plant would still leave the plant a soulless impersonal entity. But if he were there for only two days a week a worker would bring with him the knowledge that during the other three days his human skill and imagination would be used in whatever was the area of craftmanship in which he was also employed. Alternatively, if a fully automated factory required, for its running, a high degree of skill from all its workers, then the impersonality would vanish and the worker would be able to give himself in his work all the five days of the week. But he would have to realize that the interest of his work was an important part of its reward so that he could not expect to receive wages much in excess of those earned by people in enterprises which also required skill (though of another kind) and provided interest, but which were economically far less productive, if, in the economic sense, they were productive at all.

That this quick sketch is hopelessly simplistic is fully admitted. Doubtless it is simplistic to the point of idiocy. But its aim is not to suggest a programme of action (that would be like a child who had just learnt the multiplication table giving a lecture on Einstein's theory of relativity), but to provoke, even if only by deserved raillery, a discussion that could lead to a first glimpse of the possibility that things can be changed so that people may find in their work that opportunity for self-giving which is their inalienable right as God's children, and the only recipe for Joy.

Education

In this book we have drawn a distinction between two ways of knowing: what we have called Deliberation (putting two and two together and coming to a conclusion) and what we have called Intelligence (the going out to an object with all the sensitivity at our command, entering into it, and realizing it, so that it becomes included in our own personal identity).

Obviously education must include instruction in the art of Deliberation, not only the three R's but their extension in various fields of technical competence. Society could not function unless its citizens were so instructed. But there is a tendency among politicians of a certain kind to emphasize instruction of this sort at the expense of all else, as though the object of education were purely utilitarian—to make pupils into efficient cogs for society considered as a machine. The result, however, would be to produce people who would find it extremely difficult to discover God's Joy because they would be unequipped to discover themselves in the world around them. For this discovery can come only from the way of Intelligence, and Intelligence is not a matter of instruction but of evocation. Sensitivity cannot be taught. It has to be caught. And to make provision for it to be caught is the highest vocation of the teacher. He has to be the kind of person through whom his pupils may discover themselves in deep communion with their world.

And this extends infinitely beyond the mere acquisition of information (with which what is called culture is often confused). The ultimate aim of education must be to make people open to value, to find their life in it, whether the value is embodied in other people, in what people create, or in the natural world of hills and rivers. For it is only by being thus open that people can find the joy of life, which is God's Joy. And, finding this Joy, people will increase it by becoming creators in their turn, however unspectacular their creations may seem to be. In short the object of education must be to enable people to enjoy life, not superficially as passive receivers but deeply as active participants. And only by the way of Intelligence can they do this.

If what is called education is reduced to no more than instruction in the practice of Deliberation, then people are being robbed by this reduction of their inalienable human right of discovering God's Joy. And this is an infinitely worse deprivation than the exclusion of formal religious instruction from the school syllabus. For that may be no more than the letter while Intelligence is the spirit.

The complaint often made about sex education in schools, that it reduces the profundity and splendour of human relationships to the dimension of a biology lesson, is of universal application. For human life cannot be reduced to the dimension of a lesson about anything. And, in the last resort, it is for human life and its limitless patterns of Joy that young people should be prepared.

Ecology

So much has been said in this book about our communion with the natural world by the way of Intelligence that it is hardly necessary to underline what the ecologists have been telling us about our rape and ruin of the earth on which we live. This first came to people's notice in the period between the two world wars as the result of soil erosion, which sprang from the exploitation of the earth on a vast scale for commercial profit, leaving once fertile lands a desert. And it prompted T. S. Eliot in the Boutwood Lectures he gave at Cambridge in March 1939 to warn us that "a wrong attitude towards nature implies somewhere a wrong attitude towards God and the consequence is an inevitable doom".

Eliot here put horse and cart in the right order. The ultimate protest against the rape of the earth cannot be on the utilitarian grounds that the world's resources will soon be exhausted. That may be true, although it always remains possible that technology will produce alternative sources of energy when we have exhausted all those now available. The ultimate protest against the earth's exploitation is our apprehension by the way of Intelligence that the earth is the dwelling-place of God's Joy and therefore demands the forbearance, respect, reverence and love by which alone we can establish communion with Him.

The wrong attitude towards God of which Eliot spoke is that which regards Him as an object up there who lives in a kind of benevolent isolation from what He has created, a God who never walks in the garden He has planted, so that the garden may be turned into a rubbish heap without any sense of desecration or blasphemy. Such an attitude is totally impossible for anybody in whom the Joy of God has gone out to meet His Joy in the earth. Such a person will do everything in his power to preserve the Garden of the Lord from all the forms of pollution and exploitation which may threaten it, however much people tell that person to mind his own business. For it *is* his business, and everybody's.

The non-utilitarian attitude to the natural world, which enables a man to find himself there because he finds God, has been strikingly put by Coleridge:

"The first man of science was he who looked into a thing, not to learn whether it could furnish him with food, or shelter, or weapons, or tools, or ornaments, or *playwiths*, but who sought to know it for the gratification of *knowing*; while he who first sought to *know* in order to *be* was the first philosopher. I have read of two rivers passing through the same lake, yet all the way preserving their streams visibly distinct—if I mistake not, the Rhône and the Adar, through the lake of Geneva. In a finer distinction, yet in a subtler union, for the contemplative mind, are the streams of knowing and being. The lake is formed by the two streams in man and nature as it exists in and for man; and up this lake the philosopher

sails on the junction-line of the constituent
streams, still pushing upward and sounding as he
goes, towards the common fountain-head of both,
the mysterious source whose being is knowledge,
whose knowledge is being—the adorable I AM
THAT I AM."

Loneliness

The loneliness in which many individuals—and
families—live prevents them from discovering God's
Joy.

This is a state of affairs about which something
should and must be done. But it calls for much more
than active goodwill on the part of private
individuals, essential though that is. For loneliness,
and the deprivation of Joy which it entails, can
become a habit that is not easily broken. People
reach a state where they do not wish their adjust-
ment to loneliness to be disturbed. Private
individuals who wish to heal people of this social
evil need, therefore, the expert guidance of psy-
chologists, sociologists and social workers, if their
goodwill is to be effectively articulated. We need to
devise a comprehensive and informed strategy both
to bring people out of their present loneliness and
also to see that in future people do not unnecessarily
fall into it.

Such a strategy will probably not receive much
support from politicians as it is as little vote-
catching as the factory legislation which

Shaftesbury pushed through Parliament in the middle of the last century. But lonely people desperately need an amelioration of their condition, and it is not beyond the combined wit of man to provide it. "Sin", said Simone Weil, "is nothing else but the failure to recognize human wretchedness." Loneliness makes far more human beings far more wretched than the hardest of hard pornography. But there are no rallies about it in Trafalgar Square. Unfortunately it lacks the fascination of pornography.

Foolishness

One final example of how the discovery of God's Joy can be made all but impossible by the society in which we live is to be found in the absence in any set-up or enterprise of down-to-earth realism and common sense, the sort of realism and common sense which Jesus commended in the parable of the unjust steward, and whose absence in the form of foolishness he listed among the evil things which proceed out of the heart of man.

"All the grand sources . . . of human suffering", wrote John Stuart Mill, "are in a great degree, most of them almost entirely, conquerable by human effort." And the effort will require shrewdness and a realistic appraisal of the state of affairs. Only harm can be done, for instance, by treating us sinners as though we were saints and denying the present reality of what is called original sin. When a group, be it a nation or an institution within a nation, acquires power it is often assumed that its members will (or should) behave like saints and renounce the power for which they have laboured so long and hard. But, we sinners being what we are, no group of people has ever voluntarily renounced power, as Thucydides recognized over two thousand years ago. Or when a visionary idealist (Karl Marx was one) works for the establishment of a state of affairs in which people will live happily ever after in a condition of perfect harmony and goodwill, the folly of his failure to reckon with the fact of original sin will fundamentally vitiate his plans and thus cause the most terrible amount of human misery, as we can see in the tyranny of Soviet Russia today. The folly of expecting sinners to behave like saints can be found on all levels of community, not least in families where pious parents expect it of their children who consequently grow up distorted by guilt and incapable of Joy.

Common sense and realism require of us an elementary and pedestrian goodness which is willing on all levels of community to go into the fray, to check and balance influence with influence, power with power, even if in the process (since we ourselves are also sinners) we often get our hands a little dirty. A great deal can be done in this way to make conditions more propitious for the discovery of God's Joy, while the foolishness of mental masturbation in the form of idealist dreams of a totally impracticable character is sterile except in its possibility of causing unnecessary harm.

There is another form of public foolishness that is haunting because it remains so elusive. Its existence seems undeniable. Perhaps we may approach it by using as a parable a description by A. L. Rowse in his autobiography of the kind of logic which prevailed in the home of his childhood. His parents possessed a donkey which was a nuisance. If you asked, "Why do we need the donkey?" the answer was: "To carry the hay." If you asked, "Why do we need the hay?" the answer was: "To feed the donkey." It is difficult to get rid of the suspicion that a great number of our economic and social structures are based on the same sort of logic. Neither A nor B are necessary. Yet we must have A because of B, and B because of A. We must have more and more consumer goods because their manufacture provides employment. Yet the higher and higher wages their purchase demands compels firms to reduce their work-forces. To be caught up in that sort of foolishness does not make the discovery of God's Joy any the easier. There must be a way out.

Not Utopia

It has already been made clear that when we work to change society for the better we must not be beguiled by utopianism. Utopianism is a heresy because it offers us a false infinity as if the hole in the human heart can be adequately filled by anything less than God. This has always been frankly admitted by totalitarianisms of Left or Right. For both have attempted to be God to their victims, demanding of them the unquestioning ultimate loyalty which only God can demand. The state must be trusted and served even if it slays within people everything of human value.

We must try to change society for the better. But in doing so we must understand that the result will not be Utopia. For the better conditions we may successfully bring about will in their turn become corrupted and need reform.

> "We have to remember", said T. S. Eliot, "that the kingdom of Christ on earth will never be realized, and also that it is always being realized; we must remember that whatever reform or revolution we may carry out will always be a sordid travesty of what human society should be—though the world is never left wholly without glory."

If those words seem a trifle harsh we should remember the makeshift that punishment always is. "The activity of punishment", said the late Bishop Ian Ramsey, "is one which always involves us as something less than persons, whether as punisher or punished." Yet a human society without any sort of penal code is inconceivable.

Nevertheless, perhaps Charles Péguy put the matter more positively and attractively. For Péguy any real reform or revolution consisted in a return to human values.

"A revolution", he said, "is only valid if it
gives birth to a deeper humanity and a more
traditional humanity than the current humanity.
A real revolution must be truly filled with a
greater humanity, it must be more fully
traditional than the tradition which it attacks. . . . A revolution really means a search into
the inexhaustible riches of the interior life."

For Péguy reform or revolution was always a
movement of return. As Alan Ecclestone has described it: "The world and its relation to God had
to be remade again day after day. It was to this re-
creative work that Péguy gave the name *Mystique*."
And *Mystique* had always to have priority over
political expedience or *Politique*. So there was no
room in Péguy's thought for utopianism, since the
world in its political and economic structures was
always moving away from God and had always to
be brought back, and brought back, among other
things, by practical politics. God's one, continuous,
creative act, described mythologically in the Bible
as His conquest of chaos in the form of Leviathan or
dragons—"Thou didst divide the sea by the power;
thou breakest the heads of the dragons in the
waters. Thou smotest the heads of Leviathan in
pieces"—this one creative act needed to be articulated perpetually day by day in the work men did
to create a better and more just society: ". . . one
is always beginning again. Only after the Last Judgement will beginning again come to an end."

Society in its structures is always the prodigal son, who needs not only to be reminded of the Joy of his father's home, but also, in the most practical ways, to be put on the road towards it.

THE CELEBRATION OF JOY AS HOPE

A book about the Joy of God should end with a reminder of the hope which is ours. Three Frenchmen can provide it.

The first is Péguy himself:

> "Grace doesn't travel along the paths known to us. Grace takes the road it fancies and it never takes the same road twice over. Grace is free. It is the source of all freedom. When grace fails to rise like a spring of water, it may well be percolating surreptitiously."

The second Frenchman is the Curé d'Ars, of whom one biographer has written:

> "He had no formula but the sanctified vigilance of his heart which embraced everyone and allowed him to foresee and anticipate the self-surrender of each soul, to believe in each one

as Christ did, to believe in them more than they believed in themselves."

The third is Jean Pierre de Caussade:

"The effects of grace, visible to watchful eyes and intelligent minds, are nothing short of marvellous. Without method, yet most exact; without rule, yet most orderly; without reflection, yet most profound; without skill yet thoroughly well constructed; without effort, yet everything accomplished; and without foresight, yet nothing better suited to unexpected events."

Is not Zen taught by the practice of archery in which the most important lesson emphasizes that one should be able to hit the target without aiming?

Such is the man whom, in the words of the psalmist, God has made glad with the Joy of His countenance.

NOTES

page

14 ". . . strained time-ridden faces . . ."—T. S. Eliot, "Burnt Norton", *Collected Poems, 1909–62*, Faber, 1962.

15 "Thou hast made us . . ."—St Augustine, *Confessions*, Everyman, 1972, Book 1, ch. 1.

17 "No single station of the globe . . ."—Thomas Blackburn, *Collected Poems*, Hutchinson, 1975, p. 36.

19 *The Penguin Dorothy Parker*, 1977, p. 54.

20 Quoted in J. P. Whelan, *The Spiritual Doctrine of Friedrich von Hügel*, Collins, 1971, p. 60.

— "God is not far . . ."—Acts 17 : 27 & 28.

22 Thomas Merton, "Pray for your own Discovery", *Seeds of Contemplation*, Burns & Oates, 1964.

23 "I live; yet not I . . ."—Galatians 2 : 20.

— "God utters me the word . . ."—Thomas Merton, op. cit., p. 22.

— Jean Pierre de Caussade, *Abandonment to Divine Providence*, Herder Book Co., 3rd English edition 1921, p. 71.

24 "The earth is the Lord's . . ."—Psalm 24 : 1.

26 Professor Ninian Smart, Royal Institute of Philosophy Lectures, Vol. 2, *Talk of God*, Macmillan, 1969, p. 229.

— Charles Davis, *Body as Spirit* Hodder & Stoughton, 1976, p. 78.

— Dom Aelred Graham, *The End of Religion*, Harcourt, Brace, Jovanovich, Inc., New York, 1971, p. 221.

27 "Whose dwelling is the light of setting suns . . ."—Wordsworth, "Lines written above Tintern Abbey".

— For a fuller description of Russian Christianity see Pierre Pascal, *The Religion of the Russian People*, Mowbrays, 1977.

— Dostoevsky, *A Raw Youth*, trans. Constance Garnett, Heinemann, 1964, p. 351.

29 "In all our affliction . . ." Isaiah 63:9.

page

29 Dostoevsky, *Crime and Punishment*, trans. Constance Garnett, Heinemann, 1967, p. 287.

— L. A. Zander, *Dostoevsky*, SCM Press, 1948, p. 89.

30 Karl Jaspers, *Philosophical Faith and Revelation*, Collins, 1967, p. 260.

35 "in the very act. . ."—J. B. Mozley, *University Sermons*, Rivington, 1876, p. 139.

36 Simone Weil, *Waiting on God*, Fontana, 1959, p. 487.

37 Charles Gore—sometime Bishop of Oxford and founder of the Community of the Resurrection.

— G. L. Prestige, *Life of Charles Gore*, Heinemann, 1935, pp. 428–9.

39 "is apt to betray . . ."—J. B. Mozley, op. cit., pp. 176–7.

— P. N. Waggett, *The Scientific Temper in Religion*, Longmans, 1905, p. 76.

40 Geoffrey Beaumont—composer of the Folk Mass, one time Chaplain of Trinity college, Cambridge, and subsequently a member of the Community of the Resurrection. Quotation from a lecture delivered at the C.R. Wantage Week, 1966.

— "Thou blind pharisee"—Matthew 23 : 26.

41 "Do not be children . . ."—I Corinthians 14 : 20.

43 Simone Weil, *Waiting on God*, Fontana, 1959, p. 138.

— Eckhart quotation from Aldous Huxley's *The Perennial Philosophy*, Chatto & Windus, 1969, p. 324.

44 Coleridge quotation from *The Statesman's Manual*, ed. R. J. White, Routledge & Kegan Paul, 1972, p. 60.

— "I see thy light . . ." —*Scottish Journal of Theology*, Vol. 30, p. 373.

— A. Herschel, *Who is Man?*, Stanford University Press, California, 1966, p. 793.

49 Gabriel Marcel, *Being and Having*, Dacre Press, 1949, p. 129.

50 S. T. Coleridge, *Selected Poetry and Prose*, ed. Simeon Potter, Nonesuch Lib., 1950, p. 508.

page

51   "Happy is the man"—Proverbs 3 : 13, 18, 19.

—   "in every generation . . ."—Wisdom 7 : 27; Ecclesiasticus 4 : 12.

53   D. H. Lawrence, *A Propos of Lady Chatterley's Lover*, Mandrake Press, 1930, p. 54.

—   S. T. Coleridge, *Lectures on Politics and Religion*, ed. Lewis Potton and Peter Mann, Routledge & Kegan Paul, 1971, p. ix.

54   "God guard me . . ."—W. B. Yeats, *Collected Poems*, Macmillan, 1969, p. 326.

55   "the noise of passions . . ."—George Herbert Aaron, *The Temple World's Classics*, Oxford University Press, 1961, p. 165.

56   Jean Pierre de Caussade, *Abandonment to Divine Providence*, Herder Book Co., 3rd English edition 1921, p. 51.

57   Simone Weil, *Waiting on God*, Fontana, 1959, pp. 119–20.

—   Reference to St Paul—I Corinthians 3 : 21.

59   "How hardly shall they . . ."—Mark 10 : 23.

61   Rimbaud, *Oeuvres Complètes*, Bibliothèque de la Pléiade, Paris, 1954, p. 219.

62   Ralph Waldo Emerson, *The Complete Prose Works*, Ward Lock, 1909, p. 80(b).

64   Alan Ecclestone, *A Staircase for Silence*, Darton, Longman & Todd, 1977, p. 59.

—   Quoted in Marjorie Villiers' *Charles Péguy*, Collins, 1965, p. 351.

65   G. L. Prestige, *Life of Charles Gore*, Heinemann, 1935, p. 151.

67   "the logic of superabundance"—see Royal Institute of Philosophy Lectures, Vol. 2, *Talk of God*, Macmillan, 1969, p. 113.

68   Irish Murdoch, *The Fire and the Sun*, Oxford University Press, 1977, p. 45.

71   "the Body of Christ"—I Corinthians 12 : 14 seq.

page
71   "Christ in God's eternal purpose . . ."—Ephesians 1 : 10.
—   "the entire created universe"—Colossians 1 : 17.
—   "If one member suffers . . ."—I Corinthians 12 : 26.
—   For more information on Eastern Orthodox thought see
     Vladimir Lossky, *The Mystical Theology of the Eastern
     Church*, James Clarke, 1957, p. 121.
—   Thomas Merton, *Asian Journal*, Sheldon Press, 1974,
     p. 68.
—   Rupert Brooke, *Poems*, ed. Geoffrey Keynes, Nelson,
     1952, p. 131.
73   Elias Bredsdorff, *Hans Christian Andersen*, Phaidon, 1975,
     p. 91.
—   T. S. Eliot, "Ash Wednesday", *Collected Poems, 1909–62*,
     Faber, 1962.
74   Patrick White quoted in Peter Beatson's *The Eye and the
     Mandala*, Paul Elek, 1976.
75   Friedrich von Hügel, *The Reality of God*, ed. E. G. Gard-
     ner, J. M. Dent, 1931, p. 139.
76   "If you let it . . ."—John Cage, *Silence*, Calder & Boyers,
     1967, p. 139.
77   Gwendolen Cecil, *Life of Robert Marquis of Salisbury*,
     Hodder & Stoughton, 1922, Vol. 1, pp. 118–19.
79   Parable of Jesus and the farmer—Luke 17:7 seq.
80   "The Joy . . . with which Jesus endured the cross"—
     Hebrews 12 : 2.
—   J. B. Mozley, *University Sermons*, Rivington, 1876, pp.
     181–2.
82   *The Wit and Wisdom of Pope John*, collected by Henri
     Fesquet, Signet Books, New York, 1964, p. 56.
85   Reference to St Paul—Philippians 2:17.
—   *The Poetical Works of Thomas Traherne*, ed. Gladys Wade,
     Dobell, 1932, p. 232.
87   Gabriel Marcel, *Home Viator*, Gollancz, 1951, p. 28.
88   J. N. Figgis, *The Will to Freedom*, Scribner's, New York,
     1917, p. 227.

page

89 Karl Jaspers, *Philosophical Faith and Revelation*, Collins, 1967, p. 64.

90 Reference to Sonia in Dostoevsky's *Crime and Punishment*, trans. Constance Garnett, Heinemann, 1967.

— E. M. Almedingen, *An Unbroken Unity*, Bodley Head, 1964, p. 136.

91 Article by Iris Murdoch in *Encounter*, January 1961.

93 Article by Don Cupitt in *The Myth of God Incarnate*, ed. John Hick, SCM Press, 1977, p. 140.

94 Reference to St Peter—John 21 : 18.

95 Coleridge quotation from *The Statesman's Manual*, ed. R. J. White, Routledge & Kegan Paul, 1972, p. 25.

96 Florence Farmborough, *Nurse on the Russian Front, A Diary 1914–18*, Constable, 1974.

— Van Gogh quoted in W. H. Auden's *Forewords and Afterwords*, Faber, 1973, p. 298.

— P. B. Shelley, *Defence of Poetry*, ed. F. B. Pinion, Brodie, 1955.

— W. B. Yeats, *Dramatis Personae*, Macmillan, 1936, p. 89. *Patience*, Act 1.

97 Norman Douglas, *South Wind*, Secker & Warburg, 1929 edition, p. 260.

98 John Betjeman, *Collected Poems*, John Murray, 1958, p. 22.

101 Jean Pierre de Caussade, *Abandonment to Divine Providence*, Herder Book Co., 3rd English edition 1921, p. 41.

102 Reference to the woman in travail—John 16 : 21.

— G. Manley Hopkins, *Poems*, ed. W. H. Gardner, Oxford University Press, 1967, p. 100.

103 Lionel Trilling, *Sincerity and Authenticity*, Oxford University Press, 1972, p. 157.

105 D. Z. Phillips, *The Concept of Prayer*, Routledge & Kegan Paul, 1965, pp. 61–2.

— "The characteristic of the love of God . . ."—Ephesians 3 : 19.

page

105 Article by Iris Murdoch in *Encounter*, January 1961.

106 Reference to the New Testament—Ephesians 5:20.

—   "But the Christian . . ."—D. Z. Phillips, *Faith and Philosophical Enquiry*, Routledge & Kegan Paul, 1970, p. 209.

—   Simone Weil, *Waiting on God*, Fontana, 1959, p. 131.

107 Rudyard Kipling, "A Conference of Powers" in *Many Inventions*, Macmillan, 1949.

109 Reference to St John's gospel—St John 3:21.

110 "the mystery of Christ's Body"—I Corinthians 12:14 seq.; Ephesians 5:32.

—   "the weapons of our warfare . . ."—II Corinthians 10:4.

114 "In the sweat of thy brow . . ."—Genesis 3:19.

119 T. S. Eliot, *The Idea of a Christian Society*, Faber, 1939, p. 62.

120 S. T. Coleridge, Notebooks 1811–12, quoted in *Selected Poetry and Prose*, Nonesuch Lib., 1950, p. 186.

122 Simone Weil, *Gravity and Grace*, Routledge & Kegan Paul, 1952, p. 86.

—   Reference to the parable of the unjust steward—Luke 16:1–8.

—   "the evil things which proceed out of . . ."—Mark 7:22 & 23.

—   John Stuart Mill, *Utilitarianism*, Everyman, 1972, p.14.

124 A. L. Rowse, *A Cornish Childhood*, Jonathan Cape, 1935.

125 T. S. Eliot, *The Idea of a Christian Society*, Faber, 1939, p. 59.

—   Bishop Ramsey quoted in Royal Institute of Philosophy Lectures, Vol. 2, *Talk of God*, Macmillan, 1969, p. 223.

126 Charles Péguy quoted in Marjorie Villiers' *Charles Péguy*, Collins, 1965, p. 179.

—   Alan Ecclestone, *A Staircase for Silence*, Darton, Longman & Todd, 1977, p. 81.

—   "Thou didst divide the sea . . ."—Psalm 74:13 & 14.

127 Péguy: Marjorie Villiers, op. cit., p. 275.

page
127 Daniel Pézeril, *Blessed and Poor: the Curé d'Ars*, Harvill
     Press, 1961.
128 Jean Pierre de Caussade, op. cit., p. 80.
—   "God has made glad . . ."—Psalm 21 : 6.